***Anthony Hopkins*** *Academy Award Winning Actor*

*All acting should be fun.... I know some actors don't like to learn their lines too soon. But I do. I learn my lines so that I don't have to worry or think about them and that lets me be free to do the work.* Dramalogue, February 13, 1992

# Accolades!

*I am totally fearless in auditions, monologues and all my work due to Russ Weatherford's Instant Line-Learning Technique.*
KAREN DENT, ACTRESS AND AUTHOR

*My comprehension and speed increased 10-fold and allowed me to focus on the important stuff: like being the character!*
CRAIG AUSTIN, "GENERATIONS"

*Russ has the special gift for bringing a scientific precision to the knowledge of our craft. He has developed many new and innovative ideas that help the actor become more efficient and more comfortable in his work.*
RUTH WARRICK, ACTRESS
"CITIZEN KANE" & "ALL MY CHILDREN"

*This technique frees actors to do what they want to do: create and entertain.*
JIM AUBREY
FORMER PRESIDENT OF CBS AND MGM/UA

*The line-learning technique allows me to emphasize the artistic aspect of my craft without the technical getting in the way.*
RAY NORRIS
"TWISTED JUSTICE"

## Special Thanks . . .

Special thanks to Dean Regan for his many hours of backbreaking (or at least finger cramping) compiling, typing, editing, copying, suggesting, and overall "sense". All our love and appreciation to Sonja Nall for her grammar, punctuation, tense-sequencing, pronoun-usage and general "red ink" knowledge. Without her input this would have been a very discursive book. Deepest appreciation to *Moonlight Design* and David Ryer for his graphic design expertise and effort above and beyond the call of duty.

Lots of love, respect and thanks to: Ken and Valarie Grant for their support and love during the developmental stages of "the technique"; Joan See for giving this technique its first "home"; Mary Warren for her faith and encouragement; Ruth Warrick for her insight and *energy*; Jim Aubrey for his professional guidance; Craig Austin and Karen Dent (they know why). A dedication is like an Oscar speech, we could go on and on. Those who we've left out, we hope you know how much you're appreciated!

Many thanks to our partners Damon Berg, Dean Regan and Ed Wermund for allowing us to take time out of producing and running a studio to write, edit, re-write, re-edit, re-work, write again, and edit eight more times. Our deepest regards to all of our students, past, present and future, who have been patiently waiting for this book to be published. We hope it has been worth the wait.

# CONFIDENCE & CLARITY:

## The Complete Guide to Instant Line-Learning

*BY*

# RUSS WEATHERFORD

*COMPILED AND EDITED BY*
**CURTIS R. PLATTE, III**

# Dedications

*Dedicated to our families and friends,*
*Who encouraged us to strive for*
*What we felt mattered:*
*T a l e n t.*
*We love you all.*


To Connie, Mazie & Russ --

*You would have liked this one.*
*We're sorry you didn't get a chance*
*To see the final product.*
*But we know you're happy,*
*Wherever you are.*

*Love*

# A Foreword
## by Ruth Warrick

I met Russ many years ago on the set of "All My Children". He was a fellow actor, but because we rarely shared the same set, I really didn't know him very well. That changed dramatically when, by chance, we ended up being dance partners in the "Soap Bubble-Boogie Contest" held by a local New York disco. The idea was to have couples from each of the New York-based soap operas compete against each other to raise money for a local charity. The winners were to appear on a local television station to promote the charity through the dance contest. Well, Russ and I won. No one could have been more shocked than the two of us.

We were a last minute entry and had never danced together and had *no* time to rehearse. The young people on our show who had rehearsed an elaborate number "chickened out" when they saw their costumes were not as elaborate as their competitors.

I'd agreed to "save the honor" of AMC by doing an "Auntie Mame" type tango with the child actor who played my grandson, Charlie. It didn't really fit the contest, but at least AMC would have an entry.

Only a matter of minutes before the contest was to begin, before an audience of wildly cheering fans, I was informed that Charlie would not be there after all. He had recently been enrolled in a Catholic Boy's School, and the teachers did not feel it was appropriate that he be out dancing on a school night. I understood perfectly, but was disappointed. The Master of Ceremonies was also distraught, and said, "There is someone else from your show here who wants to enter the contest and has been trying to find a partner. Why don't you team up with him?" I said, "I'd love to, but I'm not a very good disco dancer, and I'm sure he is. I really don't want to embarrass myself."

Paying no attention to my excuses, he was off across the crowded room in search of Russ. Between the two of them, their enthusiasm swept me along as if it were a dare. Russ told him the music he wanted and the MC rushed off to locate the tape.

We literally only had minutes to plan our choreography, and *no* time to rehearse. As we were being announced I suddenly turned to Russ in a panic and said, "The one thing I *do* know how to play is *story line*. That's what we're going to do. I am a wealthy "older woman", infatuated with this young lover (Russ). You are all too eager to seduce me, but I am "hot" and "cold" by turns. When you're close and grab me in your arms, whisper in my ear our next move. When things get quite intimate, I'll break and dance away, and you come after me."

He nodded agreement, our music started, and we were on! *But it was not the music Russ requested!* In fact, we'd never heard it before! Actually, it was a lucky break; it began slowly and gradually worked up to a faster and faster tempo, ending in a frenzy -- perfect for our "story line". We finished to a tumultuous applause and despite some very clever numbers that had been professionally choreographed, the judges presented us with the trophy.

I'll never forget our producer, Jörn Winther, who certainly had an eye for the gorgeous young things, saying, "I can't believe it! You two really won it fair and square! You were the sexiest things I've ever seen."

That experience was a bonding one for Russ and me on several levels. First, it meant our communication was instant and deep and trusting. Next, our willingness to risk making fools of ourselves and, most importantly, our overriding desire for and passion in the act of creativity won the day. And almost always that combination will. There was vastly better *dancing* in some of the acts, but no one reached out and "grabbed" the audience's emotions as we did.

I've gone on at great length about this incident because I think it has real bearing on the content and the intent of this book.

Though it never occurred to me until this moment, Russ' whispered instructions to me were a form of "instant line-learning", and it freed me of my own self-conscious feeling of humiliation as a dancer, and empowered me to embody and radiate the story I wanted to tell. To me this is the heart and soul of this book.

I have watched with empathy and sometimes with horror at the pain and panic actors go through "fighting for lines". Often, I've been aware that even if they were letter perfect in their memorization, so much of their mind was engaged in hanging onto the words that there was woefully little energy left to throw into *playing the part*. So, they were robbing themselves of the sheer joy of being able to shift into the high gear spirit where true creativity lies. At the same time, they were robbing the audience of the thrill of resonating to the actor's projection of an essence so rich, so full, so real that the audience would have felt a powerful sense of participation.

For me, this is the whole point: to enable the audience to feel something it would not have felt, or realized, or understood had I not done my job well. However, to do my job that well, I will need to learn and practice certain techniques that will *allow* me to consistently reach that level of communication.

As Russ and I had many conversations on this subject, I began to realize that he was well aware of exactly what those techniques are, and that as a naturally born, highly gifted teacher, he should consider funnelling more of his time and talent into this field, reserving his time as an actor to roles that especially interested him.

Russ has the special gift of bringing a scientific precision to the knowledge of our craft. He has developed many new and innovative ideas that help the actor become more efficient and more comfortable in his work.

During the following years he created the line-learning technique that you are about to read and hopefully master. It is an amazingly simple and yet complete method for gaining a talent for learning lines. I was fascinated with it. Although Russ works with so many different areas of the actor's craft, this one phase seems to be the foundation of the actor's responsibility.

I was so impressed with what Russ was doing that I invited my grandson, Erik, who was at the time in high school, to spend the summer with me in New York and study with Russ. I could never have dreamt what an impact that summer would have on his life. He had a "hankering" that he would like to be an actor, (a notion that was an anathema to his parents). My attitude was, "Let's get him some good training and see what happens." He loved it from the start. He got a couple of extra roles on the soaps, and learned the exhausting experience of making rounds. But what fascinated me was the diligence with which he studied his notebook, and his lines, and boned up for his tests. Erik had never been a strong academic student, in spite of native intelligence. His grade average was not strong enough to insure his entrance into a first-rate college.

But like a miracle, after studying the line-learning technique with Russ, Erik began to use the steps he had learned to change his whole approach to education. He made straight A's his senior year in high school, and was accepted to the University of North Carolina where he continued to make A's in such varied subjects as chemistry, physics, biology, etcetera. He completed his Bachelor of Science with honors and is now working on a Master's Degree. What a great investment that summer turned out to be.

I can't emphasize how valuable I believe this process to be. It was created with a true desire to make a difference in the tools used by the actor to become a storyteller. The side benefits of being able to use the technique in so many other fields of endeavor where the learning of information is essential are also a bonus.

Russ has developed so many important teaching techniques and clarifications of the actor's needs that I was very pleased to be asked to write this forward for the Instant Line-Learning Technique. As we all know, there is no "instant" way to acquire a talent. And that is what this book does. It gives you the knowledge and repetitions that will enable you to achieve a talent for line-learning. Once that is done, it will seem that the speed with which you learn your lines is almost instant.

I wish you great success in the mastering of this information. I know that it will make a vast difference in your approach to the characters that you play, as well as the business itself. Enjoy it. It could be the beginning of achieving the greatest dreams of your life. The dream of being a storyteller. Free from fear and ready to project the power of your energy.

*Ruth Warrick*
Actress
*Citizen Kane & All My Children*
New York, 1992

# *Introduction*
# *by Jim Aubrey*

I understand the difficulty actors have with lines. Having produced many shows and having been on many sets, I have had the opportunity to see countless actors struggle with their lines. And not always without reason. With the escalating speed of production (due to financial cutbacks), actors are being asked to master more dialogue in shorter periods of time than ever before. Moreover, actors are being afforded less focused rehearsal time, in spite of increased on-the-set rewrites, line changes, and scene additions. Keeping a production on schedule is often the producer's primary responsibility. Therefore, the pressure he places on his actors can be considerable. Unfortunately, as the pressure is increased, the actor's ability to maintain his lines verbatim often evaporates.

In my estimation, millions of dollars a year are lost due to actors not knowing their lines. I have seen this factor become an increasingly important consideration in hiring, and especially in rehiring, specific actors. I have watched the speed of TV and Film production increase ten fold, while the actor's ability to learn lines has remained at the speed of theatre production.

I have seen actors "crack" in the attempt to learn, on a weekly basis, the amount of dialogue a television series demands. Sadly, producers no longer have the luxury of nurturing actors back to a place of confidence. There is no growth process on the set. The actor must develop the ability to remain in balance and in total possession of his lines outside of the working arena. The industry can no longer afford to serve as its own training ground.

Since meeting and working with Russ Weatherford and Curtis Platte, I have developed a great deal of respect for their insight, and dedicated pursuit of the truths of our business. These qualities are refreshing in an industry that is surrounded by a murky cloud of subjectivity. By determining what is provable, they have freed themselves to explore the creative.

I can only say that I wish this technique had been available twenty years earlier. As an executive producer, I would have enthusiastically suggested that every actor study it with commitment. And I suggest it now; actors deserve to enjoy their work and to have confidence in their lines despite the pressure we, producers, put them under. This technique frees actors to do what they want to do: create and entertain.

> *Jim Aubrey*
> Former President of CBS
> and MGM/UA
> Los Angeles, 1992

# *Preface*

Learning lines is not hard work. There's a trick to it. A technique. I'm going to go through each step, explaining what it is, and how it works.

One of the best parts of this technique is that it can help *anyone* who has the need to learn lines: an actor in theater, television or film; a public speaker; a politician; or a student. Anyone who has the need to learn lines in order to present himself with confidence and clarity, will benefit from this technique.

Since graduating with a Masters degree in theater, I have acted, directed, and written for stage, television and film. In addition, I have taught acting classes on both coasts. While teaching, I found one facet of acting that has been sorely ignored: line-learning. The ambivalence of most actors toward the written word is monumental. So much so, that I began to question whether or not there might be an easier method of memorizing lines than the usual boring, uncreative, rote repetition used by almost every actor today.

I realized I had a knack for learning lines, but I did not know why. I set out to break down exactly what it was that I did. How was my mind operating? I wasn't looking for a creative link. I was looking for a technical link. I asked myself the questions, "Why do I learn lines so easily?" and "How can I teach others to learn lines using my technical methods?" I also needed to discover what was considered "the norm" for most people in learning lines. How do most people do it? Why does it take so much time? And, why does the actor feel insecure about the lines even after he learns them?

I realized that learning lines was a "talent"; a talent that was as important as the creation of the character itself. One important problem to address was the anxiety and frustration that comes from thinking we know the lines and then finding that, under pressure, the mind blanks, leaving us unable to retrieve the information. It would not have been enough to find a process just for learning lines. A process was required which would support retaining and retrieving the lines, as well.

The basic steps of this process came fairly easily. Finding the structural clarity and specifics took much longer. In fact, it required a constant observation of hundreds of actors in order to isolate a technique that could be easily learned and practiced.

My discovering the easiest and most effective technique available, for this "thing" that most actors consider their "personal albatross", didn't seem to inspire many actors to try it. I wondered why. "Why are actors so reluctant to change their antiquated way of line-learning?" It seemed to me that getting the lines out of the way quickly would allow the actor to deal with the creative process of discovering his character. That should be exciting. That should be liberating. But if this were so, why would some actors be resistant to learning this new technique?

Why would an actor, who understands the importance of knowing his lines, reject discovering an easier way? I realized that many saw my line-learning technique as an indication that their craft was incomplete. It suggested that they didn't have all the answers and that perhaps they had missed something valuable in their effort to perfect their craft. This could well put an actor into a "fear position". Even though the actors would come to class fully intending to master the line-learning technique, they also seemed to need validation for their way of doing it.

Most students are receptive to change. They are ready to discover a better way of setting the lines and hence freeing themselves to explore the creative process much sooner. With the added edge of having the lines down before rehearsal, the actor is free to dig his heels in, and bring his own unique interpretation to the creative work.

Actors want to be able to listen to the director and put his direction to use quickly and effectively. Actors want to create the best character they can with all of its viable possibilities. Trying to fumble through rehearsals with script in hand doesn't allow the actor to do that. Some actors don't understand the distinction between the actor's responsibility ("Know your lines, show up on time, and don't cause trouble.") and the character's responsibility (living in "make-believe"). Many actors seem to view learning lines as part of the rehearsal process, rather than using the rehearsal time to bring the character to life.

The majority of my students increased their ability to learn lines significantly in only a six week period. In fact, when I start each class, the goal we strive to achieve is the ability to learn lines at the rate of one minute per page -- verbatim! Regardless of the disbelief they might have when first starting the process, they soon learn that it does work. The bottom line is that without applying ourselves to a goal, we will never achieve excellence. We may be good;

we may be better than average; but without practicing the steps necessary to acquire a given talent, we'll never really master it. Period.

There are seven steps to the Instant Line-Learning Technique. And the actor needs to be fluid in all seven steps. The actor's first responsibility is to look at the script objectively. Initially, the script must be understood without the nuances of subjective character choices. Those will come later when the character lives, breathes, and says the lines the way he would say them. This requires that the actor not predetermine the character's line delivery. By using this line-learning technique, the actor can have the freedom to allow the character to feel his own emotions and think his own thoughts while saying the writer's words.

While teaching, I discovered that many actors consider getting the "gist" of their lines to be acceptable. They feel that if they communicate the basic idea of what they interpret to be the writer's intended meaning, they have done their job. Wrong. As a writer, I can only say that when I have a character say a specific word, I mean that word. Not one that sounds similar or means almost the same thing, but that word. Writers usually spend a great amount of time and care on their scripts. Out of respect for another artist's work, I suggest that actors learn their lines verbatim. My technique allows the actor to do that. In fact, it ensures it.

There's a definite connection between how well an actor knows his lines and how free he is to create. With a sound technique to practice, an actor can learn a given script at the rate of "a minute a page" with total recall. Think of it. Total mastery of a script before rehearsals even begin. By using this technique, the actor develops the ability to discover all the clues the writer has left, clues that lend dimension to the character's emotional make-up, needs, hopes, fears, history, and dreams.

*Russ Weatherford*
*Los Angeles, 1992*

# *CONFIDENCE & CLARITY:*

## The Complete Guide to Instant Line-Learning

### Table of Contents

# CHAPTER ONE:
# INTRODUCTION TO
# INSTANT LINE-LEARNING

When I first meet the actors in my class, I have a question period during which I ask them who they are, what they've done, and how they feel about acting. Their viewpoints on their profession are always enlightening and, although different, essentially the same.

For the first exercise of the class I ask an actor to stand in front of the class and introduce himself by name. He talks about what he has done, how he has gotten where he is, and how he feels about the profession of acting. When he has completed, he asks the name of a second actor and then relinquishes the floor to him. The second actor gets up in front of the class and thanks the first actor by name, giving a brief recap of the first actor's statements. (For example: "Thank you, Bob. It seems you enjoyed your experience in Cleveland. I know you will benefit from the work you did at the Anson Theatre.")

The second actor then introduces himself by name and tells something about his thoughts and experiences. When he has concluded, he asks the name of the next actor and then introduces that actor to the class, relinquishing the floor to him. The third actor takes the floor, thanks the second actor by name, and then repeats something that the second actor had talked about. He then thanks the first actor by name, and also says something about that actor's statements. The third actor then introduces himself and speaks. This goes on until every actor in the class has been introduced and has spoken about himself. When the last actor goes up, he thanks every single class member by name and gives a brief comment about what each actor had talked about.

Sound incredible?

When the class begins, I tell them this is what we are going to do. They panic. Before we even begin, doubts and fears are running wild. But, by the end of this introduction period, they have found that they are capable of recalling all the names of, and information about, each of their fellow classmates. This exercise gives the class members the opportunity to realize that their own potential for recall is greater than they had ever imagined.

We have employed some basic memory techniques, and we have begun the class with the actors getting a first-hand taste of what the class will provide them. What we are working toward is an objective (factual) approach to the subjective (opinionated) concept of learning lines. The actors are often asked to differentiate the objective responsibilities of the actor from the subjective ones of creating the character. Many actors feel they should search the character's inner soul; that they must dig into the character's past to discover all the pain and suffering that have made the character what it is. It is commonly thought that what the actor does is very subjective, guided mostly by opinions which cannot be proven; it is one person's opinion against another's. I've found that the more *objective* (systematic and fact oriented) I am in my preparation for the creative processes, the more my *subjective* (creative) talents soar! Once the confusion or fear is eliminated by *objective* awareness I have done my best, most creative and most enjoyable work.

There are certain things about our art that are based *purely* on technique. These technical decisions are completely objective.

Lines are objective. They can be proven. Either we say them or we don't. Many actors prefer to get the gist of the dialogue and then just "go with the flow". Others try to get the lines *exactly* right, but sometimes fail in spite of the effort. Some actors contend: "Words are only words; it's the idea that really matters. As long as the point gets across, that's all that's important." This is a misconception. The words have been wrought by the writer to illuminate specific ideas.

We must accept the fact that even slightly different words mean different things. Saying the exact words the writer has written is necessary to maintain the clarity of the writer's intent.

True, learning lines requires effort. However, the effort required should be spent not on trying to remember pages and pages of words, but on developing the consistency and effectiveness of your line-learning process.

Interestingly, many actors who perform on the stage are far more diligent about learning lines verbatim than those who work in television and film. This could have something to do with the fact that scripts for television and film have somehow gotten the reputation of being less important as an artistic form. Some actors suggest that their respect for stage writers forces them to be far more diligent about mastering the exact dialogue. The question is, if one's process allows verbatim recall of a theater script, why would it not work as well in a medium that requires far *less* material?

What we are dealing with is accepting the fact that the way one learns lines should be consistent. To be consistent it is necessary to know how one learns lines, as well as the amount of time the process takes.

I've known many actors who have achieved great success in theater, but have had a difficult time making the transition to television and film. It seems ironic that stage actors, with their ability to learn extensive dialogue, often discover their worst fears and frustrations in film and television are related to line-learning. Even though there are fewer lines, the actors seem to have trouble grasping them. This is due, in large part, to the significantly shorter rehearsal time in television and film. This insecurity causes undue pressure and in many cases causes their minds to go blank ... and their television careers as well.

Our goal is to ensure that we do not confuse rehearsal time with line-learning time. If this has been our habit, we will run into serious trouble when our rehearsal time is cut to a minimum, as in the film and television media.

The line-learning process must be objective. There must be knowledge and consistency within the approach, no matter what the medium. The creation of the character's feelings and needs may be subjective; the character's life may be moment to moment for him; but the design and creative crafting of the story and the dialogue are predetermined. All of that information must be locked in place so that the actor can go into "make-believe". Make-believe is impossible to achieve if the actor is trying to remember his lines.

You should never have to *think* as the actor while *living* as the character. If the lines are set to memory and instant recall, there is no need for the actor to impose himself on the character's reality.

Some fear that learning the lines before the rehearsal process will "set" a line reading and thereby limit the creative process. This is only possible if the actor is using an inferior line-learning process. The fact is that the words are merely tools that the actor uses to set the framework for the actual creation of the character. There is more than one way to say a line. The process by which lines are learned should challenge the actor to discover *all* of those ways, thus *expanding* his possible interpretations.

The actor must distinguish between his responsibility to the technical requirements of his craft and his responsibility to the creation of the character and the character's world. We do not want our line-learning approach to infringe on our creative flow. We want a clear thought process with which to assimilate the information given in the script.

In the media of film and television, scripts go through many last-minute changes. The actor must assimilate those changes without infringing on the character's world. The learning of lines should be the easiest part of the actor's process. It is the only part of the process that can truly be done alone, without communicating with or making adjustments to another person. Line-learning is the foundation on which the character is built. It is the structure for make-believe. Although learning lines accurately is essential, it is not the actor's most important function. However, lines *solidly learned* allow the actor to interpret the writer's words and the director's concept; thus freeing him to go into the his most important creative achievement: make-believe.

The written dialogue means different things to the actor and the character. For the actor, it provides the clues to the character's creation. For the character, the words are his attempt to communicate in his world. *Lines are objective to the actor and subjective to the character.* Actors should find it exciting to know how long it will take them to set their lines to memory, thus, setting themselves free for the creative process.

Most people learn lines the way they have always learned them. When we look back on the first time we had to learn lines for something, we may recall that it was in the third grade for a school play. We went to our room and said the lines over and over again until we knew them. Not the entire script, but just the lines for which our character was responsible. We then went back and said the cue lines before our lines over and over again until we knew what was said before we said our lines.

Most actors still use that process today, even though they are professional actors and their financial and professional security is dependent upon the memorization of many words. It stands to reason that the ability to learn lines, separate from the ability to create a character, is of primary importance.

There is a major connection between how well an actor knows his lines and how free he is to be creative. We spend a great deal of time studying the methods of creating a character. Shouldn't we spend a certain amount of time in developing the tools that will set the character free? Combining the learning of lines with the creation of the character actually causes the actor more work. The burden, caused by not separating the two responsibilities, makes it far more difficult to achieve the character's reality. In the media of TV and film there is too little rehearsal time for the actor to further burden himself.

With a sound line-learning technique, anyone can secure his lines and acquire the freedom to explore the reality of the character. Acting is an occupation that requires massive amounts of memory work. Some actors have an instinct for learning lines; others don't.

How often is the question, "How well do you learn lines?" asked in an audition? Chances are, never. Conversely, how often is an actor (especially an unknown actor) replaced or not rehired because they slowed production time due to "going up" on their lines? Frequently. Why lose an acting job when you don't have to? And, why not learn a process that will help make you "a joy to work with" and known as a quick study, in any medium?

The line-learning technique described here is designed to enhance creative freedom: freedom from fear, freedom from frustration, and freedom to have more time to enjoy the creation of the character.

# CHAPTER TWO:
# GUIDELINES

Step One of the Instant Line-Learning Technique deals with the structure of the technique. These guidelines are the rules to be followed when learning lines. There are ten guidelines that must be learned both mentally and physically.

*Talent is a physical placement. It is the transfer of knowledge from the mind to the body through repetition.* In other words, the knowledge we acquire is transferred to the body through the act of repetition. With this technique we are working to develop a talent for learning lines with *speed* and *accuracy*. We must develop a talent for each one of the steps in the technique.

The ten guidelines have been lettered A through J, thus allowing the mind to process the knowledge quickly by using simple memory techniques. We use the alphabet because it is a built-in *filing system* that anyone can access. The filing system does not help us learn the information with greater speed; it does, however, allow us to *recall* it with greater ease. The ten guidelines are:

> *A*loud
> *B*ook down
> *C*haracter to Caricature
> *D*ialogue
> *E*verything they know you know
> *F*eet

*G*ossip
*H*ear and See everything
*I*magination
*J*ust have FUN!

The first guideline is *A*loud. We say the lines out loud to take advantage of the sense of hearing, as well as the sense of sight. This doubles the opportunity for the information to be recorded by the brain. The human brain is the ultimate computer, and along with it comes the ability to record or to play back information. While the brain is recording, it can't playback. While it is playing back, it can't record. Our goal is to train our brain to record when we want it to and minimize its playback time. Saying the lines out loud as we read them helps us maintain this control and strengthen the recording of the information.

The second guideline is *B*ook down. "Book down" means to keep the book (script) out of your hands. Since we are using our senses to record, the sense of touch works against us. If we work with the script in hand, the words and the script become connected. By keeping the script out of our hands, we do not allow ourselves to become dependent on the feeling of the paper in our hands. In other words, we may be able to learn the lines with the script in hand, but the minute we put it down, the lines could be left with it.

When we get a script, we put it into a loose-leaf notebook. The notebook allows the pages to turn easily, makes us feel more prepared, puts us in the right frame of mind for line-learning and gives us plenty of room for notes when we work on the creation of the character. It gives us a greater sense of control. It is also advisable to get a music stand to use while you are working on lines. This gives you a place to put the notebook, and provides a sense of organization and preparedness.

The third guideline is *C*haracter to *C*aricature. "Character to caricature" means that we make fun of the characters while reading the script and working on the lines. As we read the script, we gain a sense of how the characters present themselves. They come across as either pleasant or unpleasant and we begin to make fun of them vocally.

We do this for two reasons: One, we are enhancing our ability to lock into the attitudes of the characters by exploring their vocal extremes. Two, we want a clear understanding of the writer's use of words, which indicates his vision of the character's presentation. By taking the characters to caricature, we can accomplish this faster and more accurately. It clarifies "type" without the actor's emotional involvement.

Through caricature of the character, it is possible to make only broad observations and judgements about the character. The observations are the feelings that the character wants to show. Judgements, on the other hand, are the opinions we have of what the character appears to be thinking.

The most important function of "character to caricature" is the physical use of the voice and body. Remember, we are creating a "talent" for the new script. Talent, as we have mentioned, requires transferring knowledge from the mind to the body through repetition, so that it becomes muscle memory. The physical presentation of the caricature will intensify the physical process, thus accelerating the transfer of information from mind to body.

The fourth guideline is *D*ialogue. We must know all of it. Dialogue deals with knowing *ALL* the dialogue written in the scene. Not just one character's lines, but *ALL* the lines.

We want to acquire all the knowledge about the scene that we can. It is impossible to learn a story if we know only half, or less, of the story. The *words* are the actor's *clues*; and therefore it is important that the actor know all the words. We must know the complete story to be able to tell the story.

Some people think this requires *more* work. Actually, it requires *less* work. By having total knowledge of the scene, we are free to go into make-believe without worrying about the words.

The fifth guideline is *E*verything they know, *you* know. "Everything they know you know" means that every piece of information that the characters know, we do too. If any character mentions a person, place, or thing, we automatically accept that we know what the character is talking about. We've been there. We know that person. We know everything that character knows. Period.

It's a waste of time trying to figure out this information. We must accept that you know it. It is based on stock realities. Understanding stock realities means that we know that there are certain accepted stereotypical qualities about various types of characters. For instance, a corporate lawyer is expected to wear a suit, be intelligent and articulate, and have a certain amount of breeding. When something is said in the script to indicate an exception to that stock rule, the actor must then embrace that exception as a new rule for the character. Remember, the actor himself could be the exception to the rule. If the actor is not what one would call a stock lawyer, then by placing him in the role, the exception is made.

We must accept the premise that we know these characters very well. We know everything about them. Therefore, if they have been somewhere, we have been there too. If they know someone, we know them too. If they have an opinion on something, we know what it is.

Let's not confuse our responsibilities. *We* are not the characters. Remember, our jobs as actors and our responsibilities to the characters are different. As actors, we must first learn the lines objectively so that we can allow the character to bring the words to life. It is impossible to learn the lines objectively while trying to be the character. It is impossible to be objective about oneself. However, it is rather painless to be objective about others. Our relationship to the character at this point is similar to hanging out with the same social crowd. We know everything about our group of friends. We just accept the fact that we are part of the character's social world, but we are not the actual character (yet).

This has nothing to do with creativity. We simply accept that we "know" rather than "not know". The information of the scene will be clarified later by a director or by an addition to the script. We just save our questions at this stage and accept the fact that we know all.

The sixth guideline is *F*eet. "Feet" means to stay on them! We must keep moving. As we use energy to move about, we replace it with more energy. This strengthens our physical position while we work on the lines. The learning of lines should be a workout. If you don't sweat while working on lines, you're not putting enough energy into this part of the technique. Increase the energy and get on your feet!

We are involved with a physical workout that transfers information from the written page to the brain, and then to the body. It is a physical effort. The movement and the energy that are used are extremely important. Remember, it is the control of our body energies that will give us the talent for the scene that we want to acquire.

This line-learning process is designed to give us a talent for learning lines. *It is important to understand that talent for anything is achieved in the same manner. First, we must acquire knowledge. Then that knowledge must be transferred to the body through physical repetition.* This physical repetition turns the knowledge into muscle memory. By engaging the body, we free the brain. Staying on the feet builds a physical application that will transfer the information from the mind to the body with much greater speed.

The seventh guideline is *G*ossip. Gossip is generally considered a negative activity because it is used to malign and hurt people. However, in this line-learning technique, "gossip" is viewed only as a physically energized way of recounting a story. We are gossiping about characters that we know very well and dislike very much. As "gossips" we should think of ourselves as having been there when the scene took place, just like a "fly on the wall". In fact, we are such consummate gossips that the characters went to the trouble of sending us a transcript of what they actually said. (That way they know that we won't misquote them.) We should have already witnessed the scene before we ever read the script.

This *is* possible. We simply accept the fact that this is *not* new information. We were there. So, reading the script for the first time, is just a memory refresher.

There are only thirty-six dramatic situations in storytelling. They can be found in the book, *The Thirty-six Dramatic Situations* by George Polti, published by THE WRITER, INC. Once we accept this, we realize that we already know all the possibilities. The only thing that varies is the sequence of events in the characters' lives that has made them who they are.

The writer's creativity stems from his ability to make original characters that behave a certain way within the established sequence of events. The goal is to recognize the dramatic situation as quickly as possible. Thinking of the situation as gossip helps us do that faster. If we also imagine that we were there when the events in the story actually took place, then we immediately gain an upper hand on the information.

Though stage actors often have the reputation for learning lines word-for-word, they also tend to make that word-for-word line-learning more difficult on themselves.

First, most stage actors use the entire rehearsal period to learn the lines. Secondly, they almost always learn their lines in the first person, as the character. By training ourselves to learn lines more effectively, we can cut the time allotted for learning lines down fantastically. By learning the lines in the third person, instead of the first person, we take some of the personal pressure off of ourselves. The "Gossip" guideline implants the information as the third person from the outset and helps us learn the information much more quickly. Making these two adjustments in our understanding of learning will help us not only on stage, but also in television and film where the rehearsal and performance time-table is highly escalated.

We must be sure that when we approach the dialogue as gossip, we are clear on the translation of the words. English is the language that we speak. Because we speak it fluently, we often take it for granted. There are nuances and idiomatic expressions that we may not specifically understand about the scripted words. We will discuss this in more detail later, but suffice it to say that as we approach the scene as a gossip, we must make sure that we understand what the words *mean* in English.

We should ask ourselves if we would use the phrases and expressions that the characters use. If they say something that we don't understand, we should ask someone. If we don't ask, we may miss information resulting in mental blanks that will keep us from maintaining make-believe.

The eighth guideline is *H*ear and see everything. When dealing with the script, we must make sure that we don't miss the little things that the characters say: those little comments that are so revealing but are said in such a way that they appear to be unimportant. If we are not careful we will pass right over them. We hear all of what the characters say and see in our minds the picture of how they looked while they were having the experience described in the scene.

This is easy because the mind thinks in images, not words. We take the words and turn them into images so the brain can understand them quickly and accurately. We use our knowledge of "stock" information to create these images. If we do not allow ourselves to hear and see everything visually, we are creating further obstacles for ourselves that will reappear at a later time, causing confusion and frustration.

The ninth guideline is *I*magination. The human brain has an unlimited "budget". We do not have to skimp on the visuals that we create in our minds. We can let our imaginations go wild when we are creating the visual images. We mustn't be "common place". If we have decided from the script that the characters are rich, we make them disgustingly rich. If we gather that they are poor, we make them very poor. There is no middle class in our minds while dealing with storytelling during the line-learning process.

If a character is middle class, he is either a character who rose to the middle class from a poor background or fell to the middle class from a wealthy background. Our job is to make that choice based on the clues in the script and the recognition of our castable "type". If an actor looks like the type of person who was born rich then he must take advantage of that information. There are many stories where the characters are middle class, but our job is to determine whether they rose to it or fell to it. In either case, the author has probably made this choice and it will drastically effect our choices when we are developing the character. We don't worry that we might make the wrong choice. It doesn't matter. If we find something out later about the character that alters a previous belief, then we change that belief. It happens all the time; the choice may have been mistaken, the choosing was not.

The tenth guideline is *J*ust have fun. If it's not fun, then we are thinking about something else, and we are therefore doing it wrong. If we are thinking about life, bills, or anything else, we are not concentrating on the line-learning technique. This technique was developed to be fun and exciting. We need to feel secure that we know what we are doing, and are doing it proficiently. We also need to have a way to practice learning lines before we have to do it on an actual job, just like a ballet dancer uses the barre. We should work on line-learning all the time. Once mastered, line-learning should still be practiced. It frees us to be creative. It frees us to focus on the creation of the character's emotional reality. It should not be the most difficult part of our work as actors.

* * *

Spend the next week playing with the guidelines. Set yourself up with the notebook and music stand, and *pretend* that you're doing all the things that are listed in the guidelines.

Learn the guidelines. Put them into your mind so that you can practice the physical repetitions that will be necessary to create a talent for learning lines. Make sure that all the guidelines are clear to you on an intellectual and practical basis.

# CHAPTER THREE:
# BASEMAX

Step Two in the instant line-learning technique is the process by which we take the body to *Basemax*. *Basemax is the basic maximum energy that one has achieved through the repetition of a physical effort.* *Basemax* means that the energy we need to *finish* an effort is also the energy we need to *start* the effort. It may sound a little strange, but it is true.

There are many things that we have done in our lives that we did not do very well when we first started. Skiing is a perfect example. When we first start to ski, we find ourselves falling a great deal of the time. It's hard to keep focused. The energy we have for focus is minimal. But the more we ski, the stronger our energy is and the longer we are able to endure.

Once we are more proficient at skiing, when we get ready to ski we set ourselves at a certain physical level. It is a feeling. It is not a thought. We place our bodies in a position that lets us know we are ready to ski. I call this feeling *Basemax*. It is the physical position (feeling) that lets us know that we are prepared to do the best that we can do based on the level of expertise that we have. It is the level of *talent* that we have achieved.

Each person's *Basemax* is different. It may be dependant on the amount of practice we have had and effort we have made while working toward a particular goal. It keeps getting stronger as we work at it. But, if we do not focus on *Basemax*, it will not get stronger no matter how often we repeat the task. In other words, if we are only skiing down the hill, rather than focusing on increasing our competence level while skiing down the hill, our *Basemax* will not increase.

As another example, let's say we decide to do sit-ups. We get into the position to start: we lie on the floor and get ready. We do ten and find that we can't do anymore. The next day we lie down and get ready, and this time we do twelve sit-ups. The next day, fourteen. The next day, fifteen. We are strengthening our muscles through repetition, and the energy we have harnessed for the effort of sit-ups is greater than it was when we started.

Each time we begin the effort the body takes on a new feeling of control. The placement of the body is different. In effect, this is the result of the mind's ability to control the body by forcing it to do things that it doesn't want to do. We are creating a talent.

The body is working against us, but *not* out of malice. The body works on instinct. The body is the vessel in which one's life-energy exists. The energy itself, while in this body, has one primitive function: to protect the vessel in which it resides. The energy wants to keep the body in a protected position. This energy position is internal. It causes the body to remain in a "state", which is a feeling. That feeling must be justified by the mind. The mind evaluates the feeling, using the senses (sight, sound, taste, touch, and smell) and creates a thought, resulting in an emotion. When we seek to achieve a new talent, we must attempt to change the body position in order to harness the energy. Thus, we avoid the feelings that result from a locked energy placement.

The body will try to work against us. The body's instinct is to make as little physical effort as possible. When we decide to acquire a new talent, the first obstacle is to keep the body from working against us.

It is like breaking a wild horse.

Like a wild horse, the body will fight us when we are trying to master a new task or idea. Our only hope in winning the "fight" with the body is to repeat the task or new information over and over again. As the body gets more and more comfortable with the task or idea it will realize that it requires less effort to do the repetition than it does to continue to fight. If we stop too soon or are not focused in *Basemax* the body will "win". If we start working on something, and due to frustration or annoyance we give up, the body has won the battle for control of our energy. Essentially, the body has kept us from achieving our goal by *locking* our energy inside. This locked state will stop our repetitions.

It might appear that the mind, and not the body, stops the repetition. The mind is taking its cues from the body. The body's frustration, with its accompanying thoughts, leads us to believe that the effort we are working on is not in our best interest. It may be something that we really want to do, but we give up, allowing the body to control our thoughts.

There is a battle going on between the actor and himself. One warrior is the body. The body has no mind; it only deals with feelings. Its primal responsibility is to survive and to seek pleasure. The other warrior is the conscious mind. It has goals that it wants to achieve and desires it wants to fulfill. When the thoughts in the mind (caused by an intellectualization of how the body feels) conflict with the desires and wishes of the mind, then the *conflict* can be seen in the relationship *between the mind and the body*.

The mind and the body work together only when in a talent position.

*Talent is the ability to do something physically without thinking about it.* Talent requires action. Action is physical. Therefore, in order to acquire a talent, we must be physical. The process for acquiring a talent is always the same. We must first acquire the *knowledge* of how something is done, then we must find the physical action and *repeat* that action over and over. That will transfer the information from the mind to the body.

Many people believe that talent is something innate. Either we have it or we don't. If that were true, why would we need to study? Wouldn't it just come naturally? There are things for which we may have an aptitude. Therefore achieving control of those things appears to be easier. But that does not negate our ability to achieve a talent in an area that does not come easily; gaining that talent will, however, require more effort and dedication.

What have you attempted, which initially you thought you would never accomplish, but eventually mastered? First, you had a *desire* to accomplish the activity. Then you had to *repeat* the activity over and over. Perhaps others told you that there was no hope that you would ever *master* the activity. But, you didn't give up! You *wanted* it because it would get you something else that you wanted even more.

And you got what you wanted!

There is one common denominator in the pursuit of talent. We must acquire knowledge, and then put that knowledge into practical application on a consistent basis. We must practice everyday. We are practicing the placement of knowledge into the body. We are working to create the feeling of what we are doing. The feeling is *Basemax*.

We must understand what *Basemax* feels like. It is the process by which the brain overrides the body, gaining control over its effort.

There is a difference between a feeling and a thought. A feeling is a bodily sensation. A thought, on the other hand, is the mental justification/interpretation of a feeling. This intellectualization of a feeling then becomes an emotion. But, how does the body *feel* when the mind is confused?

It feels tense.

"Tense" is a feeling. That feeling is the body working against us. We are not in *Basemax*. We are not in the physical control position of acquiring knowledge. The brain is so busy justifying the body's feelings (in this case feeling tense is justified as confusion) that it cannot comprehend the task at hand.

Frustration, on the other hand, is an emotion. It is an intellectualization of a feeling. What we want to do is change the feeling. If we do, we can change the thoughts that negate our ability to learn.

It is perfectly alright to be unclear as to what all this means. It is not alright to let our own thoughts get in the way of absorbing the information that we will then use to understand the concept. Remember, we want to be able to put ourselves into a talent position. A talent position is physical. It is without fear. Fear is an emotional response to the body's desire to avoid action. Fear is the opposite of talent. So, if talent for a task can be achieved through knowledge and repetition, fear can be overcome by the same process. It is the mind's job to override the body in order to achieve action. It is from action that knowledge can be converted into talent. That talent position is what I call *Basemax*.

Remember, *Basemax* has a specific feeling. It is the physical position that we go to when we are about to work on any given effort. Once we have gone to this feeling, we can physically work on the effort. Every time we start to have thoughts of frustration or defeat, we must immediately go back to the *Basemax* feeling and continue the repetition of the effort. The next time we attempt the task our *Basemax* will be stronger, so our endurance will be longer.

*Basemax* is also a feeling of physical control, a balance. Balance itself can be practiced. It is a feeling of being grounded. Now, get up from reading this book and put your body into a *Basemax* position; a position of physical effort that you have control over. It could be weight lifting, or tennis, or skiing or aerobics. Move about the room taking yourself in and out of the balanced feeling. The goal is to have this balanced "feeling" (which you've achieved in another talent) while you do any task for which you are trying to develop a talent.

There is a test that you can use to make sure that you are in the balance position. When you are in the balance position your body will not only be unencumbered but, you will be free of thoughts of judgement or justification. You will have logical, controllable thoughts without fear. Thoughts which make our minds accessible to knowledge.

Practice it; balance is the feeling you want to be in when you are using these seven steps to line-learning. You must be in balance to be in the position of talent. It is a physical place that you can return to in order to eliminate the thoughts of frustration and inadequacy. You are working for endurance. You know your capacity to endure from the moment you begin an effort. This means by starting at your best physical level, you will always be working towards strengthening your *Basemax*. Therefore, it will become stronger and stronger. We are talking about energy.

*Basemax* is the use of body energy in a positive capacity. It is controlling the body's primal instinct: survival. It is the powerful physical action that allows one to master a talent and achieve success.

Remember, we are guided by our senses (sight, sound, taste, touch, and smell). We evaluate our feelings with our senses. When we have a feeling, the brain activates the senses to check out the immediate source of the feeling, and to determine if danger is present. In truth, the control of our energy is our "product". Energy is what we really sell. The rest is packaging.

What does all this have to do with the process of learning lines? Once we understand and can control our instrument (our body) we begin to see how it works in reference to setting and recalling information (learning lines). If we lose our *Basemax* energy, we also lose the ability to stay in make-believe, thereby going into a locked energy position. In that locked energy position, we may allow our own energy to alter our feelings. Once those feelings are altered, the brain is forced to justify or interpret those feelings. This causes the mind to have distracting thoughts which split our focus and lessen the probability of our success. We "pretend" that we are doing the activity when in truth we are just going through the paces.

What we are really dealing with are thoughts of fear. The energy is no longer in a positive position, and the results can no longer be creative.

Talent and creativity are achieved and strengthened through the use of positive energy. This positive energy is a feeling that exists when the mind and the body are working together. Our responsibility is to understand the feeling and to know exactly how it affects the mind and the talent that we are working to achieve. We need this understanding as we work toward gaining a talent for learning lines. We must be able to erase the fears that come from the thoughts of discomfort. We must realize that the thoughts are being caused by the locked energy placement in the body.

Learning lines is a talent. As a talent, it has a physical feeling or placement. It is the same type of physical feeling (placement) necessary for a talent for the audition. It is the same physical feeling (placement) necessary for a talent for the interview. It is the same physical feeling (placement) necessary for a talent for doing the job.

We need to practice this physical placement. We must be aware of how we feel. When our thoughts are negative, we must realize that our energy has reversed, and our physical feeling is different. We are no longer in *Basemax*. We no longer feel "balanced." The physical placement of being "on" is not there.

When that happens, we must alter the placement of the body and put ourselves back into a feeling of balance through control. That balanced physical placement focuses our energy and takes us out of fear and back into talent.

By going back to *Basemax* every time we have those "non-balanced" or "indicator" thoughts, we build up our endurance through repetition, which will allow us to stay in *Basemax* for longer periods of time. So, we begin to increase the length of time that we are able to stay in *Basemax*. In this case, it is for line-learning. The longer we practice and work in the balance position, the stronger our energy becomes for the practiced talent.

* * *

My specific awareness of *Basemax* has made me stronger and more proficient in the development of my own talents. As you become more acquainted with *Basemax*, I trust that you will find it practical and helpful on your road to mastering this line-learning technique and anything else you want to accomplish.

# CHAPTER FOUR:
# FRENCH SCENE

Step Three of the line-learning technique is to break down the scene or script that we are working on into French Scenes. *French Scene* is a term that has been around for hundreds of years. *A new French Scene begins every time there is an entrance or exit of a life force.* Shakespeare wrote in French Scenes, as did many of the writers in the fifteenth and sixteenth centuries. A French Scene can begin with the voice at the other end of a telephone, or a person entering after the doorbell rings. The French Scene does not begin with the ring of the doorbell, or the telephone; it begins only when there is the actual entrance of a character or a voice at the other end of the phone.

*French Scenes are the basic building blocks of storytelling.* The emotional movement of the story is totally dependant on the life energies of the characters who are brought in and out of the story.

Now, we should practice determining and marking French Scenes. After we have done this we can apply the remaining four steps to that particular French Scene before moving on to the next French Scene. (The remaining steps are discussed in subsequent chapters.)

Each French Scene has a life unto itself. Included at the end of this text is a 74-page script which is designed to help you appreciate the value of using the French Scene in learning your lines. Use the included *Workbook* as a handy text to help you learn and repeat each Step of the line-learning technique.

Go through the script and draw a line at the end of each French Scene. *Remember: a French Scene begins every time there is an entrance or exit of a life force.*

\* \* \*

Now, let's check that we are totally clear as to what a French Scene is and how to recognize it.

The script in the Workbook Tutor has been broken down into French Scenes. Take the time now to review the answers in the back of the book. I have anticipated some possible mistakes and have given explanations as to why those moments in the scene may have been confusing.

I recommend watching several television shows or feature films in order to become aware of the French Scenes in the story. I also suggest getting a play script and breaking it down into French Scenes to get a clearer understanding of the importance of French Scenes to the structure of storytelling.

I want to emphasize that it should become second nature to see when a French Scene begins and ends. While watching television, or a movie, or reading a book, notice when there is a change in the life energy, by the entrance or exit of a life force.

The French Scene will prepare us to begin learning the process that will both clarify and electrify our ability to learn lines with *speed, accuracy* and *total recall.*

In many cases French Scenes may be added by the director. In film, the prevalent theory is that the director is the author of the film. He is called the "auteur". This word is French in origin, and is based on the concept that the director moves the emotional progression of the story through his inclusion of new French Scenes or his exclusion of existing French Scenes from the writer's script.

It is important to know why line-learning is broken down into French Scenes rather than just sections or traditional scenes. The French Scene is familiar to the brain. Just like stories, every French Scene has a beginning, a middle, and an end. In addition, since you are breaking the story into French Scenes, we are processing smaller bits of information to learn.

The brain learns from top to bottom and bottom to top. So, if we create more tops and bottoms, it will be easier for the brain to learn the information. Once we move on to construction, we will create even more bottoms and tops by breaking the French Scenes down even further.

Understanding French Scenes will affect the way we approach a character. It is directly connected to the emotional reality of the character.

# CHAPTER FIVE:
# CONTENT

Content is the written word of the script. It is what the words say, *not* what they don't say. Far too often we read something into the script that is not there. What we should do is deal with what is there first. We must be careful not to add subtext to the content.

The writer is responsible for the context. The subtext is also his responsibility. Many people are misguided into believing that the actor is responsible for the subtext. The truth is, through the coloration of the specific words the writer chooses, he lays the clarity of the context and the foundation of the subtext. If one hundred different actors took the same scripts, almost all of them would say the characters were really trying to say something else: that is the subtext.

The subtext holds the deeper meaning of the script. Without it there would be little interest in the story. The dialogue is what the character uses to cover (or hide) his thoughts which have been generated by his feelings. That provides the mystery of the story.

The actor, on the other hand, is responsible for actor text. Actor text is the coloration that comes from all the collaborators' input. It is the combination of context, subtext, director text, costume designer text, etc. All the collaborators' input, in addition to the actor's individual uniqueness, and acting choices, combine to make actor text. It is the truth of what the character is thinking based on his feelings.

We are dealing with the inner workings of the characters' minds. What makes them tick? What makes them respond in a given way? These choices have been made by the writer. The information is released throughout the dialogue until we reach the climax of the story. This is true regardless of the kind of story we are telling. Through the dialogue we learn about the characters and see the way they present themselves. Each French Scene deals with a character's belief. As the audience learns more and more about the characters, through dialogue, the story is clarified.

The character clues for the actor are found in the dialogue. The director decides how he wants to tell the story. His concept determines *whose* story we are telling. He determines how the audience will follow the story, and through which character's eyes the audience will see the action. The director's concept will further clarify the nature of the character's belief system.

It's important to have a total grasp of the lines so that we have a point of reference when we go to an audition or a rehearsal. *Point of reference means: a clear understanding of the story through our comprehension of the script's written words.*

The collaborators, (the director, the writer, the other actors, and any other person who makes any major decisions regarding the project, including, the producer, and the technical support artists (such as costumers, lighting designers, art directors)) study the basic concept of the story to find the clues and exceptions to the rules which will allow for their creative input. Understanding how dialogue is used by the collaborators will make it easier to master the approach to content.

The content tells us both general and specific information about the characters. The general information refers to stereotypes. The specific information indicates the exceptions to those stereotypes, and therefore allows the audience to accept that a given character might do certain things that are out of the ordinary.

Life makes these rules. We have certain expectations of how people act based on a general understanding. This general understanding is called "type". If we look at a list of character types according to the characters' professions or life styles, each reader will have the same general idea of what each type of person is like.

Let's use the example of a woman from Beverly Hills. Would she be rich or poor? The rule is that she would be rich. The exception is that she would be poor. If she were rich, the script would not have to deal with it. If she were poor, then that fact would be dealt with in the context of the script. There are countless examples of rules and exceptions. It is the exception to the rule that makes a story different. While working on the content of a script, it is important to be aware of what the rules are so that we can recognize the exceptions. The writer makes the exceptions (i.e. describing his wealthy romantic lead as a short, unattractive, eccentric man) and the director makes adjustments to those exceptions as presented by the writer to clarify the story to the audience. This is an important part of the collaborative effort. All the collaborators must share specific knowledge of the *story*. This will lend a clarity to the final product which will illuminate the rules and their exceptions within the world of any given story.

In the Gossip guideline we used our imagination to recount a scene in a highly energetic "gossipy" fashion. We pretended that we were there when the scene took place. We know these people and everything about them. Knowing them makes the story more important to us.

We are not reading the script from the character's point of view. We are reading it as an observer. As an observer we are not one of the participants in the scene. Our intention in reading the script is to obtain every point of information in the French Scene.

The who, what, when, where, and why of the scene are the points of information we want to assimilate from this reading. With the script sitting on the music stand, we will read through it and then walk away from it. As a third party (gossip), we tell an imaginary fourth party (person) the major points of information in the French Scene.

For example, say that the scene has two characters in conversation. That makes them the first and the second parties. We are the third party observers, and the imaginary person that you are talking to is the fourth party.

To repeat: after reading through the script, we walk away from it and as a third party, tell an imaginary fourth party what the French Scene is about. You cover the who, what, when, where, and why. If the answer to the who, what, when, where, and why questions are not in the content, we make it up. Using our general knowledge of the scene and stock realities, we fill in the information not given in the script to answer the questions.

If we make the wrong choice we will be given the new information at a later date and it will replace anything that we have made up. The purpose is to detail the information at hand. If we don't do this, we will leave so many holes that we'll become confused, allowing us to fall out of *Basemax*. We may allow these doubts and missing pieces of information to be excuses for negative thoughts.

The mind has an incredible capacity for absorption. It will retain information as long as it actually records what it has read. If, when we walk away from the script, we can give the points of information, the brain has successfully recorded that information. If we can't, it didn't. If the information was *not* successfully recorded, we probably were not in *Basemax*. In fact, we may have been talking to ourselves -- in our minds -- while we were reading the script. Even though we were reading the words out loud, we still might have managed to have that internal conversation.

If we have set ourselves in *Basemax* energy, and we are on our feet, moving, saying the lines out loud as we read the scene, and we are taking the characters to caricature, then we are training ourselves to record what we are reading.

It is imperative to keep our energy up and stay confident. If we don't have the points of information, then we reset ourselves, go back to the script, and read it again. Employ all the guidelines. After we have read the scene again, we walk away and, again, as a third party tell a fourth party the points of information. For example, let's take Act 1, Scene 1 on the first page of the workbook. Our points of information would be: The scene is between Don and Carolyn. They are in a police holding room. Don thinks Carolyn is trying to blackmail him. Carolyn wants Don to help her and is going to use some past information to have him come through. Carolyn says she's terrified, and Don says everything is circumstantial. Carolyn says she knows what the police have and it's not good. She has a record, and she brought Kathleen to St. Michaels. She says she will not confess to something she didn't do; Don says she should just wait, or she will hang herself. (Note: Stop there even though the scene continues because it is the end of the French Scene.)

When we can get through the points of information, we are ready to move on to Step five. If we are not ready, we go back to the script and go through the process again. We continue to do this until we know the points of information. If we have only a general understanding of the points of information, we will regret it later. Knowing the content is the foundation of this process; not knowing will only cause trouble.

It is important to realize how powerful the mind is and what it is capable of understanding. If the mind is in the right position for recording information, it can record a great deal. If we were to read a novel, we would find that we could go into great detail about the story for anyone who asked. We could recount a whole novel after only one reading!

Let's take another example. If we read a magazine article that seems like it would be of importance to someone we know, we would file that article in our mind. A week later, when we see the person we had thought about while reading the article, we would be able to recount the article's points of information ... after only one reading.

Another example: We overhear a conversation about someone we know. We could repeat that information to someone else weeks later even though we only heard it once. The mind will record the contents of the scene after only one reading. What is most important here is that the mind is set in the "record" position. If the information is of importance the mind will be more receptive to assimilating the information and will set itself into the "record" position.

While we are the third party, telling the fourth party what went on in the scene, we must be sure to make observations and judgements. *The observations are the things that we actually heard them saying, as well as how they said those things. The judgements are how we felt about what they said and how they said it.* These observations and judgements are very important. We must visualize and use our imagination. Remember, we were there!

Also, remember, that English is a language to be translated. Even though it is our language and we speak it fluently, we can not presume that the translation is clear in our minds. While reading the script the first time through, we read each thought independently. We do not connect them to each other. We ask ourselves if we would use that thought or expression in our own lives. If so, we move on. If not, we make sure that we understand the thought or expression. We ask someone, if necessary. If not, we are leaving a blank in the brain that will eventually lead to confusion and lack of control.

# CHAPTER SIX:
# CONSTRUCTION

We are going on to Step Five: Construction. The word construction means the way something is put together. In this step we break the script down to the basic elements of structure. This has nothing to do with the structure of the story itself, but of the information in the script.

As we said before, the brain is the ultimate computer. It records information and then organizes it for access, based on how that information was received.

A computer system has three basic elements. The first is the Central Processing Unit (CPU) which is the computer itself. The CPU holds the basic information that has been built into the computer. The second element is the software program. That would be, by our definition, one's "talent". That is a specialized program designed to fill the need for a specific function. The third element is the file. That is the information that is created with the use of the CPU and the specialized programs (software). You keep that information on a separate disc. This separate disc is called a file.

Our computer (the brain) is our CPU. It already has the general information of life that allows us to function as human beings. It has all the information that is directly related to us. It has our beliefs and memories, as well as our relationships to everything and everyone we have experienced. Those things are what make one person different from another, and they are also what make people the same.

All human beings have a great deal of the same information. We work from the same biological structure. It is our personal experiences that create our individual beliefs. Those beliefs alter the way we relate to the things and forces around us.

Software packages are specialized tools which our CPU is accessible to. They are our talents. We all have varying numbers of talents (or software packages) for our computer. Some people have more than others. Some people are too busy trying to understand their "CPU" to deal with developing numerous software packages. However, everyone has some. We may not recognize those "software packages" as talent, but that's what they are. These are the things that we can do without thinking; things that we can do without stress or discomfort.

When someone is working with one of their talents, each new project within that specialty becomes a file. That file is the information specific to the new project and is integrated with the software package. In this step (construction) we are setting up a "file" in the line-learning "software package". Understanding the construction helps to clarify and organize the script in our mind. Understanding how to use this construction file is integral in comprehending this line-learning process.

When we are working on a script in order to learn the lines, we use our talent (software package) for line-learning to create a new file for the specific script that we are learning. The new file is the organization of the information in that scene. Each French Scene is put onto that file. After we have put the information of the lines and their structure on that file, it becomes the major file for that project. From then on, every piece of information regarding that project is recorded on that same file. The interview, the audition, the rehearsals, and the performances all become part of it. It continues to build and maintain all the information needed for that project.

If we allow ourselves to work in this structured way, we will not have to deal with the personal fears of our "CPU". But, if we put information in our CPU without organization, we will mix that information with our personal knowledge and beliefs. So when we want to retrieve that information, we will run the risk of accessing unnecessary or negative information that may interfere with our achieving *Basemax* or from retrieving the information that we want.

Having completed Step Four (content), we then break the French Scene into a beginning, middle and end. This makes the script information more accessible. We will do this by dividing the French Scene into three equal parts. We then draw lines after the beginning, and after the middle. The rest of the French Scene will be the end. To repeat: *this is done in three equal parts*.

This will simplify the effort for the talent of line-learning. The brain learns from top to bottom and bottom to top, working its way to the middle from those two positions. French Scenes which are broken into three equal parts have more tops and bottoms and less distance to the middle. Therefore, the brain can work faster.

By breaking the French Scene into a beginning, a middle, and an end, we can structure the French Scene so that it is familiar to the brain. Most traditional scenes (scenes that have not yet been broken into French Scenes) have a beginning that deals with the formalities of the relationship, regardless of what that relationship may be. The middle is the meat of the scene; what is really going on within the relationship. The end is the resolution. This is how stories are told. The mind is aware of that structure. By breaking down the French Scene, remembering that a French Scene is a story unto itself, we can provide the brain with a feeling of familiarity.

We are not dealing with the words. We are dealing with the construction. The brain is not evaluating the information for content. It has already done that. At this point, it is dealing only with construction.

Remember, construction is for structure and organization. After we have broken the French Scene into a beginning, a middle and an end we will work with each section independently until we can recall all the information within that section.

Now, flip back to the workbook and use it as we go over the example. The script has been numbered down the side of the page to give quicker reference.

We will work with Act 2, Scene 1. It should already be broken down into four French Scenes. Note that the first three French Scenes occur at line 13 on page 15, line 11 on page 16, and line 18 on page 16. We will use the fourth French Scene (from line 1 on page 17 to line 5 on page 22). Break it into a beginning, a middle, and an end.

We will now work with the beginning section of this French Scene. The beginning section ends at line 12 on page 18. First, we count the total number of "speaks" in this beginning section. *A speak is the dialogue one character says until that character is done, or is interrupted.* Each time we see a character's name above the dialogue, we call that piece of dialogue a "speak". The first speak is Don's. The second speak is Dean's. The third speak is Don's. The fourth speak is Dean's. This pattern continues to the end of the section.

We are now going to count the speaks out loud using our fingers as counters, in consecutive order. While we are counting the number of speaks in the beginning section, we will also say the lines out loud, employing all the guidelines. There are eleven speaks in the first section of the fourth French Scene in Act 2, Scene 1

After we have finished counting the speaks, we go back to the beginning of the French Scene and count the number of "thoughts" that each character has each time he speaks. *A thought is any grouping of words that ends in terminal punctuation.* (e.g. ellipsis (three periods), period, colon, double dash, semi-colon, exclamation point, or question mark.)

Now, go back to the beginning section and count the number of thoughts that each character has when he speaks. In Don's first speak, he has one thought. Then, Dean has one thought. Don has one thought. Dean has one thought and then follows with another thought. This continues until the end of the beginning section of this French Scene, which is Don's speak, "And...".

When we count the speaks, we count consecutively to the end of the section. When we count thoughts, we begin a new count within each speak. After we have counted the speaks, and the thoughts, we forget about the numbers and move on. Do not underestimate the mind. It has already used the numbers to organize the file. It is ready to move forward.

In the beginning section there are eleven speaks. The number of thoughts varies from one to three. The purpose of counting is to set up a filing system for the brain. After we have read the scene and counted the speaks and thoughts aloud, we step away from the script. As a third party, we again tell an imaginary fourth party the sequence of events told within the conversation.

For example, we walk away from the script and say, "Don said, 'What happened to you last night?' Then Dean said 'What do you mean?' Then Don said 'You came home and went directly to your room without a word'." We continue to say the dialogue, verbatim, until the end of the beginning section. If a character says more than one thought in a speak, such as line 17, page 17, we will say, "Don said, 'Dean, I brought you into my home.' And then he said, 'If you're having a problem, I need to know what it is.' And then he said, 'Well, what is it?'"

Our goal is to learn the sequences of thoughts verbatim (word for word). This will not only allow us to have a confident handle on our scenes, but it will make sure that we have an opportunity to use the writer's words clearly, thus helping us to illuminate our character as closely as possible to the writer's intent.

If we can't remember the next sequence of thoughts, we go back to the top of the beginning section and read it again. When we get to the line that we do not recall, we make a strong visualization, and then continue to read through the rest of that section. Remember, the mind thinks in images, not words. Visualizing with a stronger image will set the sequence of thoughts better. We walk away from the script, and once again, as a third party, tell an imaginary fourth party, the sequence of thoughts in this section. If we can not recall a thought, we repeat the process remembering to make strong visualizations at each trouble spot.

After we have gone through the beginning section without referring to the script, we repeat the same process for the middle section. We count the speaks, and then the thoughts. When we walk away from the script, we repeat the sequence of events to a fourth party using the "he said-she said" (or "he said-he said", in this instance) approach. Each time we cannot recall a thought, we go back to the top of the section and reread that section aloud until we come to the thought which we could not recall. We make a strong visualization (remember, we were there) and then read the rest of the section. Now, we walk away from the script and repeat the process until we can go through the entire middle section without returning to the script.

Before going on to the third section, we repeat the process combining the first and second sections. Once we can get through the sequence of events of both sections together, without dropping a line, we are ready to move on to the third section. We use the same process with the third section; and, when completed, link all three sections together, by starting at the top of the French Scene and doing the "he said-she said", third party to fourth party process through the entire French Scene.

If we cannot recall a certain thought, we go back to the top of the French Scene and read down to the thought that we could not recall. We make an even stronger visualization, and then read to the end of the French Scene. We do this each time we can not recall a thought until we can get through an entire French Scene verbatim without returning to the script.

Remember we are still following the ten guidelines. We are still adding our observations and judgements, and we are having fun telling the story.

At first it may seem to take a lot of time, but once we start working with the process we will see that the thoughts will come much more quickly than one might imagine. The more we practice the process, the faster the lines will come.

Each time we return to the script and read to a point that we cannot recall, our minds correct the words that we may have misplaced (or misused) in the thoughts that we *were* able to recall. This built-in correction device cleans up any incorrect phrasing as we reread the script, and it finds the thought that we could not recall.

Practice the line-learning process through Step Five (construction) for at least twenty minutes a day. Stop at this point in the book and, using the scenes that have been provided in the workbook, practice the process through Step Five. If there's a problem, refer back to the chapter that contains the information that you need.

\* \* \*

The lines must be secure or our fears will keep us from functioning at *Basemax* when we perform the scene. The few seconds that it takes to count the speaks and thoughts allow the brain to organize the file so that it can receive the information. This is the foundation for everything else that we will do on the project.

Please put the information in this book into practice while reading it. Remember, knowledge is important. But knowledge without repetition (through action) accomplishes nothing.

# CHAPTER SEVEN:
# CONTINUITY

Step Six is continuity. According to the dictionary, continuity means "a continuous series or succession; unbroken, coherent whole". So, when we use the word "continuity" with regard to line-learning, we are talking about the movement of the thoughts in a logical progression. We are dealing with the keys that are necessary to retrieve information that has already been recorded.

We are thinking of the brain as a computer, the line-learning technique as a software package, and the script as a file. So, we must understand how our file works.

The file is where we have stored the information of the lines from the script. We have stored the lines along with additional information from our observations and judgements about the scene(s). By going through Step Five, we have placed the information on the file. Our next job is to program a code, or the keys, that will trigger our brain to retrieve the information immediately. We need a way to make the file retrieve the information on demand.

Let's employ some basic memory concepts. In the continuity step, we are going to use associations. We have all used associations to different degrees. In the Step One guidelines, the alphabet was used as an association to the information. The A corresponded to "aloud", the B to "book down", the C to "character to caricature", and so on.

If someone said, "D" in reference to Step One of the line-learning technique, we would know they were talking about "dialogue". Once the word "dialogue" comes to mind, we are able to explain the guideline. These letter associations are not meant to record the information. They are used as keys to accelerate recall. Hearing the letter allows the brain to bring the information up to the screen. The "screen" is another computer part. When we want to work on a file, we put the disk that contains that file into the computer. We punch in the key information which gives us access to the file or the section of the file that we want to see.

The associations in Step Six are the keys that are going to be used to retrieve the information from our computer (brain). These associations connect one *thought* to another *thought*.

Many people have the mistaken opinion that associations are used for memory. Associations are used for recall, not for memory. The information should already be understood and filed away. If we have gone through Step Five successfully, then we have already filed the information of the scene. We now want to have access to that information without having to think about it.

Associations are made from thought to thought. The thoughts happen in a particular sequence, following a certain pattern that has been prearranged by the writer. Each thought triggers the next thought. Look at the script at the end of this chapter. Notice that when a character has a thought, he will either have another thought following that first thought, or he will say nothing until another character speaks. If the character has more than one thought we make associations between the thoughts in that speak. When the speak is over, we make an association between the last thought in that speak and the first thought in the next speak. Each thought has within it something that activates the next thought. These are catalysts. We already know what the thoughts are. Now, we want to activate the thought without having to *think* about it.

We do not want to be required to think as the actor. We want to have access to the information of the scene by simply listening as the character. By making associations from thought to thought we can activate the thoughts without having to think of them. This will give us the security of knowing that we can go into make-believe with the assurance that the character will have all the information he needs for the scene, without the actor needing to supply it for him. If the information has been programmed properly, and the associations work, the recall will be complete and instantaneous.

There are four types of associations. The first one is called "exact" association. With exact associations there is a word in one thought that is repeated in the next thought. In Act 3 on page 36, line 19, Jana's second thought is, "You want some more pasta?". Then Ray's next thought is, "I've got pasta up to my eyeballs." The word "pasta" in the first thought is repeated in (associated with) the second thought. Since it is the same word, the association is called an *exact association*. The exact association is the easiest of the four. It is the most logical. The writer's use of exact associations makes it easier for the actor to recall his dialogue. Media that require large amounts of dialogue, but have little rehearsal time, often take advantage of this association.

The second type of association is *letter to letter* (alliteration). If there is a letter used in a word in one thought and the next thought has a word that starts with the same letter, those letters might be used for the association.

On page 36, line 8, Ray's thought is, "This is not exactly what I had in mind when I said we should have a Saturday lunch." The next thought is Jana's. She says, "I'm sorry, Ray." We use the word *Saturday* in the first thought, because it starts with an "S", and the word *sorry* in the second thought as the association. We are using a letter association in the first thought to activate the recall of the word in the second thought that begins with the same letter, "S".

We are using the association to activate the word that will then activate the thought. If the association is strong, the activation will be so immediate that we may not even realize that it happened.

Associations should work in accordance with each actor's way of thinking. No one can make an association for someone else. The important thing to remember is that the associations are what give us the freedom to recall. Each thought must connect to the next. The connection must be made by association.

If one thought has nothing in it that connects to the next thought (as in an exact or alliteration association), we use an *abstract association*. We take a word, usually the most active word, from the first thought and the most active word from the next thought and put them together in a little story.

Look at line 15 on page 38. Jana says, "Now, what would you like for dessert." Then Ray says, "You sound pretty good to me." I would take the word *dessert* in the first thought and the word *pretty* in the second thought to make an *abstract* association. Create a little story that relates to your life, or that is easily understood by the actor, *not the character*. For example: I love *desserts*, especially when they are *pretty*. If I'm going to have a *dessert* it had better be *pretty*. Of all the *desserts* I've had, and I've had a lot of *desserts*, I always liked the *pretty* ones the best.

That little exchange of thoughts is an example of using abstract association to connect the word *dessert* to the word *pretty*. Once that connection has been made, the file will give us the correct dialogue. Remember, an abstract association must be personal to the actor using it.

The fourth association is called *substitution association*. In the event that we realize that we have been substituting a word in the script for another word that is similar but not the same, we would use the substitute association to correct the mistake.

On line 7, page 38, Jana has the line, "Not many people would have been as gracious." If we realize we have been saying, "Not many people would have been as nice," we make a little story to replace the word "nice" with the word "gracious". It is done exactly like the abstract association. For example: "I've been nice all my life, but I've never been able to be gracious. I've always admired people who were gracious because it is much classier than being just nice. If I could choose between nice and gracious, I would take gracious, hands down." Remember, two words often have similar, but not exact, meanings.

These are your keys. They are very important. You will have the chance to see what a difference associations make in Step Seven: the line-learning test. If we took the line-learning test after Step Five, we would not be able to pass it. But, after we have made the associations, our recall is much stronger.

Now, go through the script with a pencil and circle each word that is going to be used as the association word. Do that until the entire French Scene has been gone through. Every single thought must have an association. Once that is done, we're are ready for Step Seven.

Remember, *every* thought has to be activated. That means that the first thought in the scene must have a thought before it to activate it. Since there is no written thought before the first thought, we make one up. We give the character who has the first thought a "pre-thought" that will activate the first thought. For example, on page 8, line 15, Deena has the opening line, "Why did you call me Deena?" We should make an internal line of dialogue that reads, "I wonder why she called me Deena." That is the line we say to ourselves at the top of the scene to activate the written line.

At this point we are only dealing with the *Basemax*. We need not deal with the guidelines, although we should still be on our feet and speaking aloud to keep our energy and focus up, and to keep us in *Basemax*.

Take the scenes that are provided in the workbook and go through the process through Step Six. Make sure that a strong emphasis is put on the associations in the continuity section. Once you have done this with repetition you'll be ready to continue the book.

# CHAPTER EIGHT:
# LINE-LEARNING TESTS

*Talent is achieved through acquiring knowledge and putting the knowledge into the body through repetition.* At this point, we have placed the knowledge in the brain (and hopefully into the body). Step Seven (the line-learning test) allows us to make sure that the knowledge has been firmly planted in both.

Before we go on to Step Seven, let's take another type of test. These are questions from the process. Write the answers down on a piece of paper.

Answering these questions will let you know if you have a clear and confident understanding of the learning techniques discussed here. The questions "should" be easy to answer. And, as each question is presented, take time to elaborate on the answer. If it is difficult to answer the questions, go back and review the information to solidify your understanding. Before going any further review the chapter(s) that covers the information missing from our "software package". Remember, if we have not "processed" the information of each step, then practicing the process will be nearly impossible. So, here are the questions:

What is the Actor's responsibility?

What is the Character's responsibility?

What is *Basemax* and how do we get there?

What is a French Scene and when does it occur?

How do we break a script into French Scenes?

What is the "he said - she said" exercise?
In what step is it used? What is it's function?

Where do we deal with the "what" of a scene?

What is "abstract" (in relation to this technique)
and where is it used?

What is the "file"?

What is the "CPU"?

What is Step One? What is A-J? Why is each
important?

What are the four types of associations?
For what are they used?

That's the test. How did you do? Assuming you passed with flying colors, let's now work on the first French Scene in Act 4, Scene 1 (page 42) from the back of this book. Spend no more than twenty minutes on it to file the scene and set up the "keys" to retrieve the scene. Apply the first six steps over the next twenty minutes. When that is finished, continue on with the book.

* * *

Now that we have had a chance to file the script in our computers, let's move to Step Seven: the instant line-learning test. This test is a confirmation of what is in place and what is not. It is for our benefit so that we can be completely confident that we have filed all the information necessary for the character to retrieve without the actor having to provide it for him.

Ask someone to you a thought (or speak) from anywhere in the French Scene. It can come from any of the characters. It could be in the middle of a series of thoughts belonging to one character. Then, respond with the next thought. If the thought belongs to the same character, then say his next thought. If the next thought belongs to another character, say that (first) thought. If a new speak is given, say the entire speak that follows.

The line test gives us the confidence of knowing that we do not have to think to retrieve the lines. The character will be thinking, but not about the "lines". He will be thinking about how to deal with the person he is with, or the situation that he is in. He is feeling too much passion or pain to actually be thinking of words. And, because of the line test, we won't have to put our friends and loved ones through the misery of "running" a scene with us. (They know from experience that when they correct us, it only makes us crazy.) And, they aren't being asked to *act*. They are just providing a line check.

It will impress them that we have acquired a system that gives us such a complete control of the script. The line-learning test also requires us to listen. If we are trying to "think ahead", the process won't work. Therefore, we must listen in order to retrieve.

We practice listening by using the phrase "What did you just say to me?". When we are going through the line-learning test and draw a blank, chances are that we did not actually hear what was said. More than likely, we used our old habit (thinking ahead) and did not hear what was said because we were listening to ourselves trying to think of the next line.

When this occurs, it is a sign that we have lost our *Basemax*. We have lost our physical placement/balance. If we go blank, we say to the person giving the test, "What did you just say to me?". At the same time, we change our body position back to that feeling of confidence (*Basemax*). More than likely, we will now hear them and the line will come. If it doesn't, we ask the person what the next thought is. We evaluate whether we knew that piece of information. If we did, we must now make a new, and a better association to trigger the retrieval of that thought. If we did not know that piece of information, (or somehow we did not read it), or never filed it, (1) go back and file that information, and (2) make an association.

Practice the process through all seven steps. Continue working on the *Basemax* exercise in addition to using it on the process.

Here's another exercise. Work on your endurance; see how long you can stay in a scene. To do this, we practice fifteen minutes a day with any scene we have learned. We do this by being *all* the characters and going through the scene over and over again until the fifteen minutes is up. If we "go up" on a line while we are doing this, we immediately become the character who is listening (not the character who dropped the line). We maintain our balance and, as the listening character, start to question the character who was supposed to be talking. We ask him why he stopped talking. What is wrong with him? We were talking about this or that and all of a sudden he just shut up! Why? What's going on with him?

By doing this, we are allowing ourselves to stay in the scene and not get trapped by our own doubts, fears, or frustrations. As soon as the other character wants to rejoin the scene, then we become that character and continue with the exercise by going through the scene.

Have fun with it! We can do the scene in many different ways. We can change the character's accents, we can make them smarter or dumber; we can do anything we want to as long as we maintain the scene. We can do it as fast or as slow as we like. This is where "character to caricature" can really help us out. It's a fun and creative way to further solidify the learning of your lines. It is also keeps us from settling into line readings.

The idea is not to think about the lines, but to deal only with the characters and who they relate to one another and *let the lines come effortlessly*. Our main objective is strengthening endurance. We want to see how long we can stay in the energy of the scene without falling out of it.

It is only through the action of discipline that we can move on into the more creative (and fun!) mode: *talent*. Discipline is the action of repeating foreign tasks or ideas until they become understood by the body and the mind. This discipline "forces" the body to work for us -- not against us. The time for discipline is always "now". It will bring with it great rewards. We must structure our time using the same methods that we have structured our technique for learning. Eventually, if we are persistent and consistent, the discipline of the technique will pay off in the talent.

Once you incorporate this step you'll see an enormous difference, not only in your work, but also in how you feel about your work.

# CHAPTER NINE:
# A FINAL WORD

You, the actor, are an independent company. You are a freelance company. You "job out". That means you, as an independent business, hire out to other companies in order to do a job. There are many tasks that you must accomplish yourself without expecting someone else to do it for you. You must have a clear understanding of what it is that your company needs and wants.

You have to know your company's strengths and weaknesses so you can take advantage of them. You must find an action to take that will turn your weaknesses from a liability into an asset.

You need to organize your time in such a way that you know you are spending it wisely. You must think as an employer; not as an employee. You own your business. Its success is totally up to you. You must search out the kind of people that will enhance your efforts. You can not waste time on efforts that, in effect, are just spinning your wheels.

If you owned your own company you would spend a good seventy to eighty hours a week working toward your company's success. You would organize that time in a way that would *best* promote your company and, even though it may take a great deal of effort, soar you toward success. You would also be aware of what you were doing to support those efforts and what you were doing to sabotage them. Inaction is action in reverse. Its results are just the opposite of the results of action. Think about it.

If you are spending a great deal of time complaining about what is not available to you, then you are working with inaction. The way to change that is through action. Action means doing something physically; using your body as your army. Once you come up with your strategies, put them in motion. Don't deal with the things you can't do, only the things that you can do. The more you do them, the closer you will get to those things that once seemed out of reach.

Once you have mastered the line-learning technique, you will have elevated your thoughts of accomplishment. You will have eliminated a major source of fear. You will have taken charge of an area that had previously kept you inactive. You will discover that it has opened the door to remove other fears that are in your way.

Talent is what you desire as a professional actor. That all-inclusive word really requires many talents in order to achieve your goals.

There is no mystery as to why one person succeeds and another doesn't. It is all a matter of action. You may not be able to start where you want to start. You may not be able to get to the people you want to get to. But that must not stop you. There is a place where you can start, and there are people who will see you. They may not be the ones you are ultimately after, but they can afford you the opportunity to practice your physical control. That physical control will allow you to acquire the talents that will get you where you want to go.

One of the most difficult things for people to understand is the power of their minds when in harmony with positive energy. Both of the words "energy" and "talent" cause many people to go into a locked state. It's as if these things really don't exist except in some philosophical way. The truth is that they are as real as rain, and as abundant as air. And they are accessible to anyone who wishes to have them. They are our birthright. No one can take them away unless we allow them to be taken. But if we do not know what we are doing, if we do not know that we have a choice, if we do not know that making the choice requires action, if we do not know that action is physical, then we will not be in touch with all the power there is around us.

It is said that "knowledge is power." The acquisition of it is achieved through action. I have labeled the physical feeling achieved through clear and confident action: *Basemax.* The exact application of that physical feeling is dependant on what effort we are working toward. It could be learning lines; it could be creating a character; it could be interviewing an agent; it could be performing a role. It could even be baking a potato.

It is through action that we are able to accomplish the intermediate steps which will then satisfy our life goals and desires.

Whatever we do, we must make sure we do not allow ourselves to get frustrated. That negative thought is the body keeping us away from action. We must take charge of our lives by being what we want to be, doing what we want to do, achieving what we desire to achieve. All of those words are words of action. They are not words of thought. We must find an action in order to practice and strengthen our talents.

* * *

I hope that you have enjoyed this book. I hope that you have acquired the knowledge and exercises that will allow you to take a stronger hold of your career. We are the masters of our fates. It is an old expression, and it is true. We *can* achieve it all, but the acquisition requires that we work at it. Concentrate on the action; reap the rewards.

# GLOSSARY

**ACTOR'S JOB**     Know your lines, show up on time, don't cause trouble.

**ACTOR TEXT**     What the audience finally sees. It is the combination of Context, Subtext, Director text, all the collaborator's input, and the actor's own uniqueness.

**ASSOCIATIONS**     Words, pictures, or ideas which are formulated to trigger a specific response. In line-learning, the association is input to trigger the next thought.

**BALANCE**     The feeling when in *Basemax*.

*BASEMAX*     The basic maximum energy that we have achieved through the repetition of a physical effort.

**BOOK**     Script.

**CASTABLE TYPE**     What type of character, by nature of one's bone structure, voice, and body, one would be cast as. Based entirely on look and stereotype.

| | |
|---|---|
| **CHARACTER'S JOB** | To live in make-believe. |
| **CHARACTER TO CARICATURE** | Make fun of the people in the scene. They are not you; they are not your friends; they are very amusing people that you enjoy mocking. |
| **COLLABORA-TORS** | All persons involved in telling a story. They include, but are not limited to: everyone on the set, all pre-production personnel, the producer, the director, etc. |
| **COMPUTER** | The brain. |
| **CONSTRUCTION** | How something is put together. In line-learning: the system created to break the information into manageable chunks which can be filed for recall. |
| **CONTENT** | The ingredients or items of something. In line-learning: the written word and Step Four. |
| **CONTEXT** | What the words mean in English. |
| **CPU** | Central Processing Unit. A computer term that, for our purposes, refers to the area of the brain where the |

information that allows us to function in our normal day to day life is stored. It is the center of our individual rules of life.

**CUE LINES**

The thought before a character's speak. Not used in this technique.

**DISCIPLINE**

Synonymous with action. It is the brain's ability to override the body's desire to do nothing. It is through discipline that repetition can be employed to achieve a talent.

**ENERGY**

The substance that differentiates between the living and the dead. The life force of all living entities.

**EXCEPTION TO THE RULE**

The foundation of the story. It gives the characters interest value, and it gives writers the ability to create an infinite number of stories within the realm of the thirty-six possible choices.

**FEAR**

An intellectualization of a feeling that resulted from energy being locked inside the body. An illogical position that negates talent, and is the antithesis of talent. Talent cannot exist while in a fear position.

**FRENCH SCENE**      The basic building blocks of story telling. A French Scene occurs with each entrance or exit of a life force.

**JUDGEMENTS**      What we feel is *really* happening in the scene. The intellectualization of our feeling about the scene that becomes an emotion. That emotion becomes a judgement based on our rules for life.

**K + R = T**      Knowledge plus repetition equals talent. It is the formula for acquiring a talent for *anything*.

**LOCKED ENERGY POSITION**      The position in which our energy is trapped in the body, causing the mind to justify feelings it receives as negative.

**MAKE-BELIEVE**      The world in which the character lives. Anything that is a technical problem for the actor (such as lights, acting to a camera, blocking) must become part of the character's world so that the character can function in make-believe without the actor thinking.

**MEDIUM**      For our purposes: Film, Television, or Theater.

| | |
|---|---|
| **MIDDLE CLASS** | Boring, nondescript lifestyle that does not relate to line-learning. It is not colorful enough. |
| **MUSCLE MEMORY** | The ability for the body to remember without the mind being present. It is the memory inherently used while in talent. It is the result of the repetition of knowledge through a physical effort. |
| **OBJECTIVE** | A piece of information that is provable. |
| **OBSERVATIONS** | What we see happening. |
| **PACKAGING** | You. What you look like, how you dress, etc. It is what the buyers see which allows you to be "typecast". |
| **POINTS OF INFORMATION** | The who, what, when, where, and why of the scene. |
| **POINT OF REFERENCE** | Having a clear understanding from a specific standpoint. In the case of line-learning, it is understanding the written word and recognizing which of the thirty-six dramatic situations the writer has employed. |

**PRODUCT**  What an actor (or anybody) really sells: the feeling other people have when near you. See energy.

**RULE**  See stock information.

**SOFTWARE PACKAGE**  Synonymous with talent. It is the individual disk that houses the information for a specific task. By setting up a software package we eliminate all the negative information housed on the hard drive, thus keeping ourselves out of a locked energy position.

**SPEAK**  Any number of thoughts a character says. A speak ends when a character is through, or is interrupted by another character's dialogue.

**STATE**  Position when energy is trapped in the body. The result of a state is intellectualization, which results in emotions of frustration, anger, annoyance, etc.

**STOCK INFORMATION**  Pieces of information that are assumed to be common knowledge to everyone. Could be thought of as stereotypes.

**SUBJECTIVE**      A piece of information that is opinion and therefore unprovable.

**SUBTEXT**      The writing in-between the lines. It is what the audience should feel the characters are really saying. It is determined by the coloration and word choices within the writing, and is, therefore, the responsibility of the writer. The actor's creative input is termed "actor text".

**TALENT**      The ability to do something (physically) without thinking.

**TERMINAL PUNCTUATION**      A period (.), question mark (?), colon (:), semi-colon (;), double dash (--), ellipsis (...), exclamation point (!), or the start of another speak.

**THOUGHT**      Any line of dialogue ending in terminal punctuation.

**TYPECASTING**      The ability for others to see, from a packaging position, what a specific actor sells. It is invaluable to have the ability to be typecast, and then use one's product (energy) to overcome the limitations that typecasting can create.

# THE
# INSTANT
# LINE-LEARNING
# TECHNIQUE
# SYNOPSIS

## *Basic Assumptions of this Technique*

Talent is the ability to perform a task physically
without thinking about the process.

Talent is only acquired one way:
Knowledge + Repetition = Talent

The body must be defeated to gain a talent.
It is the mind's ability to make the body work against it's
own will that instills the discipline for the repetition.

## THE SEVEN STEPS OF THE
## INSTANT LINE-LEARNING TECHNIQUE

**STEP #1:** *Apply these rules for steps one through five.*

    A.  Recite the words **ALOUD.** Use as many of the
           senses as possible.
    B.  **BOOK DOWN!** Do not hold the script.
    C.  Take all **CHARACTERS TO CARICATURE.**
           You don't like any of them. They are either
           sickeningly sweet, or terribly bad.

D. You are responsible for all **DIALOGUE.** Do not pay more attention to one character than another.

E. **EVERYTHING THEY KNOW, YOU KNOW.** Assume that you know everything about these people. You know what they know.

F. Be on your **FEET** and moving. Make sure your energy is working for you.

G. You are the third person -- a **GOSSIP.** You are NOT a participant! Keep yourself out of the scene.

H. **HEAR** and see everything again. Visualize. Your script is a transcript of something you witnessed. Check your transcript for accuracy.

I. Use you **IMAGINATION!** Your mind has the ultimate budget. Spend the money!

J. **JUST HAVE FUN!**

**STEP #2: *Position your body at Basemax (Balance).***

**The basic maximum energy achieved through the repetition of a physical effort requiring endurance.**

Think of your brain as the *ultimate* computer. It is. Insert a blank, floppy disk into your computer, the brain. All information about the project on which you are working is saved on this disk. Each time you work on that particular project (i.e. interview for the role, first audition, etc.) new information is put onto that disk. By placing yourself in *Basemax*, you stamp on the floppy disk: FOR PHYSICAL USE ONLY.

**STEP #3:** *Analyze the script for French Scenes.*

A French Scene occurs with each entrance or exit of a life force. Lines are learned by French Scenes.

**STEP #4:** *Content. Points of Information.*

> Who are these characters to each other?
> What do they talk about?
> When does this scene take place?
> Where are they?
> Why are they doing this?

Make Observations and Judgements.

> Observations:
> * What did you see happening?
> * What did they say to each other?
> * How did they say it?
> * What did they *want* each other to see?

> Judgements:
> * Did you believe what they were saying
>   > *OR*
> * Did you *feel* that they were hiding something?
> * What did you *feel* was really going on?
> * Did you *feel* they were honest or dishonest?

Walk away from the script and, as a third person, tell an imaginary fourth party what was going on in the scene.

Mention all points of information *in any order.*

   *THEY TALKED ABOUT ...*

Don't forget to visualize. Remember: *You were there!*

*Repeat step #4 until all information points are clear.*

**STEP #5:** *Construction: Sequence of Events.*

Create a filing system for your computer (brain).
The story only happened one way.
Only one thing happened first; then another thing happened second, etc.
Break each French Scene into three equal parts: *beginning, middle, and end.*

This is done to help the brain absorb the information faster. The brain retrieves information top down and bottom up. By making more tops and bottoms, it is easier for the brain to retrieve the middles.

Work with each section (beginning, middle, and end of a French Scene) separately, until the sequence of events is clear.

Count the speaks of the section, and then count the thoughts. After counting, *do not think about the number.* It is just a filing system for the brain, and the brain has already used that information. Simply do it, forget it, and move on.

Walk away from the script and as a *third party* tell an *imaginary fourth party* what you saw *chronologically*. Tell it thought by thought by simply filling in the blanks created for your filing system.

Make observations and judgements as you tell the story. (Keep in mind what belongs to you and what belongs to the script!)
Be colorful and imaginative.
Tell the story in the sequence of events as they happened.

**IF YOU CANNOT REMEMBER THE NEXT THOUGHT, YOU MUST:**

- Go to the beginning of the *section* that you are working on.
- Read the words *aloud* as you say what you saw.

**AT THE POINT THAT YOU COULD NOT REMEMBER THE LINE:**

- Visualize something happening.
- Read through to the end of that section.

*Repeat that process until you can fill in each thought. Then repeat the process with the middle and end sections of the french scene.*

**STEP #6:** *Continuity -- setting catalysts for retrieval of information.*

Using associations to set the key word in each line will trigger the key word in the next line of thought.

Types of Associations:
- EXACT -- word to word
- ALLITERATION -- letter to letter
- ABSTRACT -- active word to active word, connected by a story
- SUBSTITUTION -- new word to old word, connected by a story.

**STEP #7:** *The Instant Line learning Test.*

Purpose: To insure that you know all the thoughts without having to think about them.

Ask someone to read *any* thought or speak from *any* character. When you can give the following thought or speak consistently, the lines are mastered.

This simple test is to prove you have the lines in place, can retrieve them at will, and will effectively negate your fear of lines while performing.

# WORKBOOK

**CONFIDENCE & CLARITY:**

*The Complete Guide to*
*Instant Line-Learning*

1                    *ACT 1 SCENE 1*

2 (POLICE HOLDING ROOM. DAY.)

3                         DON

4 Have you lost your mind? If you think

5 that you're going to blackmail me

6 into ...

7                       CAROLYN

8 I have no intention of blackmailing

9 you into anything. You got me into

10 this mess, and if you think that I'm

11 going to keep quiet about it you're

12 wrong.

13                        DON

14 One thing has nothing to do with the

15 other. The police have no knowledge

16 of our little adventure. Whatever

17 they have on you concerning Kathleen

18 has nothing to do with me.

1                    CAROLYN

2 There's where you're wrong. It has

3 everything to do with you.

4                    DON

5 Carolyn, I know that you're

6 frightened about all this ...

7                    CAROLYN

8 Frightened? That's the understatement

9 of the year. I'm terrified! I'm

10 accused of killing someone. I didn't

11 do it.

12                    DON

13 If that's true, then you have nothing

14 to fear.

15                    CAROLYN

16 Oh, that's easy for you to say, Don.

17 You're not the one accused of murder.

18

1                    DON

2 You don't even know what the police

3 have against you. You'd be better off

4 keeping your mouth shut and waiting

5 to find out what evidence they have.

6                  CAROLYN

7 I know what evidence they have. They

8 know that I brought her to St.

9 Michaels. They know that I gave her a

10 phony resume.  And, they know that I

11 have a police record.

12                   DON

13 One thing has nothing to do with the

14 other.

15                  CAROLYN

16 They seem to think that it does.

17 Kathleen was killed as a warning. I

18 know it, and so do you.

1                           DON

2 I don't know anything of the kind.

3 You're gonna make a big mistake if

4 you don't start getting control of

5 yourself. Now, for once in your life,

6 listen. Everything they have against

7 you is circumstantial. There is

8 nothing that will hold up in a court

9 of law. They're trying to get you

10 spooked -- trying to make you

11 confess.

12                         CAROLYN

13 I will not confess to something that

14 I didn't do. Whoever killed her is

15 setting me up. Well, they won't get

16 away with it.

17                         DON

18 You'd better listen to me, Carolyn.

19 Keep your mouth shut. Wait 'til all

1 the facts are in, and then you'll

2 have a chance of dealing with your

3 defense. If you don't, you're gonna

4 hang yourself. (DETECTIVE WILSON

5 ENTERS.)

6                    DETECTIVE WILSON

7 Who gave you permission to see Ms.

8 Vallacie?

9                    CAROLYN

10 Stop calling me that. My name is

11 Carolyn Costa.

12                   DETECTIVE WILSON

13 Call yourself what you want.

14 "Vallacie" is what we have on your

15 police files and that is what it's

16 going to be. I want to know what

17 you're doing here, Don?

18

1               DON

2 Carolyn is an acquaintance of mine.

3 She called me for advice.

4               DETECTIVE WILSON

5 Are you her attorney?

6               DON

7 No, I am not.

8               DETECTIVE WILSON

9 Then, I'll have to ask you to leave.

10              CAROLYN

11 Wait one minute ...

12              DON

13 That's alright, Carolyn. I'll speak

14 to the District Attorney about this.

15 (TO DON.) If you'll excuse me.

16              CAROLYN

17 Don, wait ...

18

1                    DON

2 Don't worry, Carolyn. You'll be just

3 fine. I'll talk with you later. (HE

4 EXITS.)

5                    CAROLYN

6 You are very rude, Sergeant.

7                    DETECTIVE WILSON

8 It's "Detective", and I'm sorry you

9 feel that way.

10                   CAROLYN

11 When am I getting out of here?

12                   DETECTIVE WILSON

13 Not any time soon. I'll get the

14 matron to take you back to your cell.

15                   CAROLYN

16 Detective, wait ...

17                   DETECTIVE WILSON

18 Yeah?

1                    CAROLYN

2 (PUTTING ON HER CHARM.) I didn't do

3 it. You must believe me. I'm

4 innocent. I'll do anything to prove

5 that to you. Anything.

6                    DON

7 Nice try, Ms. Vallacie. The only

8 person you have to prove it to is the

9 judge. Have a nice day. (HE EXITS.

10 CAROLYN IS LEFT THWARTED, YET AGAIN.)

11 CUT TO:

12                    *ACT 1 SCENE 2*

13 (JANA'S APARTMENT. DAY.)

14                    DEENA

15 Why did you call me "Deena"?

16                    JANA

17 Stop it, Deena. I don't know what

18 you're trying to do, but it won't

19 work.

1                    DEENA

2 I'm not trying to do anything.

3                    JANA

4 You're just digging a hole that

5 you're never gonna get out of. Stop

6 it, while there's still time.

7                    DEENA

8 I'm Ruth. My name is Ruth.

9                    JANA

10 Your name is Deena. Deena Murphy. I

11 know it and so do you. I want to help

12 you, but I can't if you continue to

13 lie.

14                    DEENA

15 (BREAKING INTO TEARS.) What am I

16 gonna do? Please help me.

17

1                    JANA

2 Calm down. Now, let's just talk about

3 this. It's too late to worry about

4 what you've done. We have to figure a

5 way to get you out of this.

6                    DEENA

7 I'll just say my memory came back.

8                    JANA

9 You can't use a lie to replace a lie.

10 That's just gonna cause more trouble.

11                    DEENA

12 How did you know?

13                    JANA

14 Yesterday, when Dean was here, I

15 knew.

16                    DEENA

17 I don't understand.

18

1                    JANA

2 It was in your voice ... your eyes.

3 You knew how much you were hurting

4 him. Ruth could never have known.

5                    DEENA

6 I'm such a fool. Why did I want to

7 hurt him like this? I love him Jana,

8 I really do. I'm so sorry. Oh God,

9 I'm sorry.

10                    JANA

11 So, now what? What do you want to do?

12                    DEENA

13 I know exactly what I'm gonna do.

14 (SHE GETS UP AND STARTS TO HEAD FOR

15 HER ROOM.)

16                    JANA

17 Where are you going?

18

1              DEENA

2 To get dressed. I've got to make it

3 right. (DEENA EXITS.)

4 CUT TO:

5              *ACT 1 SCENE 3*

6 (HOSPITAL WAITING ROOM.)

7              NATALIE

8 You're frightening me. Oh God, he's

9 not ... Please he's not ...

10              WES

11 No. He's not dead. But, he has

12 suffered traumatic injuries.

13              NATALIE

14 What kind of injuries?

15              WES

16 He's suffered major head and spinal

17 injuries.

18

1                    NATALIE

2 Oh, my God. Does this mean he's going

3 to be crippled?

4                    WES

5 It's too soon to tell. We still have

6 tests to run. My immediate concern,

7 however, is his loss of blood.

8                    KEVIN

9 What about transfusions?

10                   WES

11 Unfortunately, it's not that simple.

12 Damon is AB negative.

13                   NATALIE

14 AB negative? What does that mean?

15                   WES

16 It means it's extremely rare. We were

17 able to have one pint transferred

18 from Chicago General.

1                    KEVIN

2 Surely, Chicago General has more than

3 one pint of AB negative.

4                    WES

5 As I said, it's extremely rare. We

6 have a call out for donors, but we

7 really haven't got any time.

8                    NATALIE

9 Well, isn't there someone in St.

10 Michaels with that blood type?

11                    WES

12 Not on record. If his parents were

13 alive, at least one of them would

14 have to have AB negative. But, as his

15 records show, both his parents are

16 deceased.

17                    NATALIE

18 Can I see him?

19

1               WES

2 I'm sorry, Miss Gardner. That's

3 impossible. Excuse me. (EXITS)

4               NATALIE

5 Kevin, I don't have AB negative.

6               KEVIN

7 So, Malcolm must.

8 (CLOSE ON NATALIE.)

9 FADE TO BLACK

10               *ACT 2 SCENE 1*

11 (DON'S APARTMENT. DAY. DEAN COMES

12 DOWN THE STAIRS INTO THE LIVING ROOM.

13 ROBERT ENTERS FROM STAGE RIGHT

14 CARRYING AN ARRANGEMENT OF FLOWERS.)

15               DEAN

16 Is Don home?

17               ROBERT

18 No.

1               DEAN

2 Do you know where he is?

3               ROBERT

4 He went out early this morning. He

5 didn't say when he would be home.

6 Would you like some lunch?

7               DEAN

8 No thank you. I've got to get to

9 class. I'll have something at the

10 cafeteria. (DON ENTERS.)

11              ROBERT

12 Good morning, sir. Would you care for

13 lunch?

14              DON

15 No thank you, Robert. I'll call you

16 if I need anything.

17              ROBERT

18 Very well, sir. (ROBERT EXITS.)

19

1                   DON

2 What happened to you last night,

3 Dean?

4                   DEAN

5 What do you mean?

6                   DON

7 You came home and went directly to

8 your room without a word.

9                   DEAN

10 Oh ... I was just upset about

11 something.

12                  DON

13 Anything you want to share?

14                  DEAN

15 It's no big deal.

16                  DON

17 Dean, I brought you into my home. If

18 you're having a problem, I need to

1 know what it is. (DEAN HESITATES.)

2 Well, what is it?

3                    DEAN

4 I went to see Deena.

5                    DON

6 You what?

7                    DEAN

8 I had to, Don. I love her and I need

9 her to know it.

10                   DON

11 And ...

12                   DEAN

13 When she didn't recognize me, I

14 pretended that I didn't know her.

15                   DON

16 Oh, Dean ...

17                   DEAN

18 I had to. I was afraid she'd hate me.

19

1                    DON

2 And what happened?

3                    DEAN

4 We got along great. She even took me

5 to the country club to help me get a

6 job as a bartender.

7                    DON

8 Dean, are you crazy? You expected to

9 go back to the place where Deena was

10 hurt to get a job? What in the world

11 were you thinking?

12                    DEAN

13 I know. It was stupid.  And I mean

14 really stupid.

15                    DON

16 What are you saying Dean?

17

1                    DEAN

2 Deena's aunt was there and she ...

3 she ...

4                    DON

5 She what!?!?

6                    DEAN

7 She hit me.

8                    DON

9 Dean, I can't believe this. Do you

10 realize that this whole thing could

11 blow up in your face?

12                    DEAN

13 I didn't mean to ...

14                    DON

15 It doesn't matter what you meant. The

16 damage is done. You have to swear to

17 me you will not go near her again.

18                    DEAN

19 I can't do that.

1                    DON

2 You not only can, but you will. Until

3 the charges have been dropped against

4 you, you will not see her again.

5                    DEAN

6 I already have.

7                    DON

8 When?

9                    DEAN

10 Yesterday. I had to tell her

11 about ...

12                   DON

13 About what?

14                   DEAN

15 I can't.

16                   DON

17 Tell her about what?!?!

18

1               DEAN

2 (BEAT.) Our child, damn it.  Our

3 child.

4 (CLOSE OUT ON DON.)

5 CUT TO:

6                *ACT 2 SCENE 2*

7 (DAYNA'S BEDROOM. MORNING. DAYNA HAS

8 HER HEAD COVERED UNDER THE SHEET.

9 SONJA ENTERS.)

10              SONJA

11 Mother? Mother. Are you going to get

12 up?

13              DAYNA

14 Leave me alone.

15              SONJA

16 (PULLING THE COVERS AWAY FROM HER

17 HEAD.) Mother, this is silly.

18              DAYNA

19 Just leave me alone.

1              SONJA

2 (PICKS UP A BOTTLE OF SLEEPING PILLS

3 SITTING BESIDE THE BED.) Oh, my God!

4 How many of these did you take?

5              DAYNA

6 (LOOKING AROUND TO SEE WHAT SHE IS

7 TALKING ABOUT.) One. (SHE TAKES THE

8 COVERS AND PULLS THEM BACK OVER HER

9 HEAD.)

10              SONJA

11 Are you doing this because of Martin?

12 (DAYNA BURIES HERSELF DEEPER UNDER

13 THE COVERS.) Mother, Martin has his

14 own life to lead. He'll come to his

15 senses. Let him do what he has to do.

16              DAYNA

17 I don't want to talk about it. Just

18 get out of here.

1                      SONJA

2 I am not getting out of here. (SHE

3 PULLS THE COVERS BACK.) Now, I want

4 you to get up and pull yourself

5 together. You have things to do.

6                      DAYNA

7 Let someone else do them. Martin has

8 ruined all my plans.

9                      SONJA

10 What plans?

11                     DAYNA

12 (TRYING TO GET THE COVERS FROM

13 SONJA.) It doesn't matter anymore.

14                     SONJA

15 Of course, it matters. Talk to me.

16 What plans has Martin ruined?

17                     DAYNA

18 (SITTING UP IN BED.) I wanted Martin

19 to find a nice wife and you a

1 wonderful husband. Then you would all

2 start raising families right here in

3 St. Michaels. I wanted us to have a

4 real family that celebrated birthdays

5 and holidays. I just wanted ... (SHE

6 BEGINS TO CRY.)

7                    SONJA

8 Oh, Mother. (TAKING DAYNA IN HER

9 ARMS.) I'm sorry. Please, don't cry.

10 Maybe it will still happen. Maybe

11 he'll come home and ...

12                    DAYNA

13 No, he won't. He's gone. I know he

14 is. He'll find that woman and marry

15 her and I'll never see him again.

16                    SONJA

17 You're making too much out of this.

18 He'll be back. I know he will. (THE

1 PHONE RINGS. SONJA GOES PICKS IT UP.)

2 Yes, Alice. (PAUSE.) Just tell

3 whoever it is that Mother will call

4 them back. (PAUSE.) What! Oh, my

5 God ...

6                    DAYNA

7 (SITTING UP QUICKLY IN BED.) It's

8 Martin. Something has happened to

9 Martin.

10                    SONJA

11 (TRYING TO HUSH HER MOTHER AS SHE

12 FINISHES LISTENING TO THE

13 CONVERSATION.) Yes, thank you. (SHE

14 HANGS UP THE PHONE.)

15                    DAYNA

16 What? Tell me!

17                    SONJA

18 It's Damon. He's been seriously

19 injured in an accident.

1                DAYNA

2 Oh, no! (SHE GRABS HER ROBE AS SHE

3 GETS OUT OF BED.) Where is he?

4                SONJA

5 He's having emergency surgery. (SHE

6 GRABS HER HEAD IN PAIN.)

7                DAYNA

8 I know he'll be alright. (SHE TRIES

9 TO COMFORT SONJA.) Get hold of

10 yourself. Come on, I have to get

11 dressed and we'll go to the hospital.

12                SONJA

13 Why? I don't want to go to the

14 hospital.

15                DAYNA

16 We have to go see about Damon. What

17 is wrong with you?

18

1              SONJA

2 There is nothing wrong with me. If

3 you want to go to the hospital then

4 go but ... Oh! (SHE GRABS HER HEAD

5 AGAIN.)

6              DAYNA

7 Sonja, are you alright? (SHE DOES NOT

8 RESPOND.) Sonja, answer me.

9              SONJA

10 Hurry up. We have to get to the

11 hospital.

12 (CLOSE ON DAYNA.)

13 FADE TO BLACK

14              *ACT 2 SCENE 3*

15 (DON'S APARTMENT. DON AND DEAN ARE

16 STILL ARGUING.)

17              DON

18 I can't believe that you and Deena

19 had a child.

1                    DEAN

2 But, she gave it up for adoption. I

3 didn't know. I want my child back. I

4 want them both back. I want us to be

5 a family.

6                    DON

7 Were you married?

8                    DEAN

9 No.

10                    DON

11 Listen, Dean. You're setting yourself

12 up for a terrible fall.

13                    DEAN

14 No!

15                    DON

16 Yes, you are. You have no legal right

17 to that child.

18

1                    DEAN

2 But, I'm the father.

3                    DON

4 I know how you must feel. But,

5 please, forget about this. There is

6 nothing that you can do about it.

7                    DEAN

8 I can't forget about it. I can't!

9                    DON

10 Dean, I promise I'll do anything that

11 I can to help you. But you are going

12 to have to accept certain truths.

13                   DEAN

14 I don't have to accept anything. It's

15 my child. Nobody asked me. I have

16 rights, too.

17                   DON

18 You're not going to get anywhere

19 until you learn to calm down. We'll

1 think of something. Try to get

2 control of your feelings and deal

3 with this in a rational manner.

4 (ROBERT ENTERS.)

5                       ROBERT

6 Excuse me, Mr. Croft. Your lawyer is

7 here to see you.

8                       DON

9 Thank you, Robert. Give me a minute

10 and then send him in. (ROBERT EXITS.)

11                     DEAN

12 I have to get to class. (HE STARTS TO

13 EXIT.)

14                    DON

15 Dean.

16                    DEAN

17 Yes?

18

1                       DON

2 Don't do anything irrational. We'll

3 figure something out. Alright?

4                      DEAN

5 Sure. (HE EXITS. DON WATCHES HIM

6 LEAVE. ROBERT ENTERS WITH MARK.)

7                       DON

8 Hello, Mark. I wasn't expecting you

9 this morning.

10                     MARK

11 Sorry I didn't call first. I have a

12 few things that we need to discuss.

13                      DON

14 What is it?

15                    ROBERT

16 Would you care for something before I

17 leave?

18

1              DON

2 No, nothing. (ROBERT EXITS.) Well,

3 what is it?

4              MARK

5 (HE OPENS HIS BRIEFCASE AND TAKES OUT

6 A FOLDER.) I need you to sign these

7 papers.

8              DON

9 (TAKES THE FOLDER.) What are they?

10             MARK

11 Sundae had a special account in

12 Switzerland.

13             DON

14 Sundae had a Swiss account?

15             MARK

16 Yes, she was a shrewd business

17 person. She diversified her

18 inheritance into T-bills, stocks and

1 some dealings that were, shall we

2 say, different.

3                    DON

4 (LOOKING AT THE FIGURES.) My word.

5 This is beyond the other monies she

6 had?

7                    MARK

8 Yes.

9                    DON

10 I can't believe this.

11                    MARK

12 Well, it's true. Just sign both sides

13 of the document and then the money

14 can be released. (DON TAKES A PEN

15 FROM HIS JACKET AND BEGINS TO SIGN.)

16 There is one small problem.

17                    DON

18 What kind of small problem?

19

1                    MARK

2 She never claimed the money.

3                     DON

4 Meaning?

5                    MARK

6 Meaning there is going to be quite a

7 large tax fee.

8                     DON

9 Oh. Is there anyway around it?

10                    MARK

11 I'm afraid not. It will eat up about

12 70 percent.

13                    DON

14 Seventy percent?

15                    MARK

16 I wouldn't worry too much. It'll

17 still keep you in pocket change for a

1 few hundred years. (DON SIGNS THE

2 PAPERS.)

3 CUT TO:

4                    *ACT 3*

5 (JANA'S APARTMENT. RAY AND JANA ARE

6 HAVING LUNCH AT THE KITCHEN COUNTER.)

7                    RAY

8 This is not exactly what I had in

9 mind when I said we should have a

10 Saturday lunch.

11                    JANA

12 I'm sorry, Ray. I just don't want to

13 leave the house until I know what's

14 going on with Deena.

15                    RAY

16 I was just kidding. I'm having a

17 great time.

18                    JANA

19 Thank you. You want some more pasta?

1                    RAY

2 I've got pasta up to my eyeballs.

3 Thanks, anyway.

4                    JANA

5 You didn't like it.

6                    RAY

7 I did like it. I think you're being a

8 little touchy.

9                    JANA

10 (SHE STARTS TO REMOVE THE PLATES.) I

11 know. I really am sorry. It has just

12 been such an unbelievable morning.

13                    RAY

14 Because of Deena?

15                    JANA

16 Yes. I can't tell you what it was

17 like. I've never spoken to anyone

1 like that before. I should have just

2 stayed out of it.

3                    RAY

4 Wrong. You did what you had to do.

5 Stop feeling guilty. She's lucky that

6 she has someone like you to care

7 about her. Not many people would have

8 been as gracious.

9                    JANA

10 I just know where she's coming from.

11                    RAY

12 Meaning?

13                    JANA

14 Meaning ... meaning I understand what

15 she's going through. That's all. Now,

16 what would you like for dessert?

17                    RAY

18 You sound pretty good to me. (HE GOES

19 OVER AND PUTS HIS ARMS AROUND HER.)

1                    JANA

2 Very funny. I didn't know that I was

3 on the menu.

4                    RAY

5 Well, now you do. (HE STARTS TO KISS

6 HER WHEN DEENA COMES INTO THE ROOM.)

7                    DEENA

8 Oh, I'm sorry.

9                    JANA

10 (TO DEENA.) Forget it. Where did you

11 go? I've been worried about you.

12                   DEENA

13 I went to the police station.

14                   JANA

15 The police station? Whatever for?

16                   DEENA

17 I had to make something right. At

18 least it's a start.

1               JANA

2 What about Natalie?

3               DEENA

4 I went by her house, but no one was

5 there. I'll call her later. I'm

6 really very tired. If you'll excuse

7 me I want to lie down.

8               JANA

9 Deena, what you are doing is right. I

10 hope that you know that.

11               DEENA

12 I know. Now I have to deal with my

13 mother.

14               JANA

15 Your mother?

16               DEENA

17 I didn't tell you? She's coming to

18 St. Michaels. I'll talk to you later.

19 (SHE STARTS TO GO TO HER ROOM AND

1 THEN STOPS. CROSSES TO JANA AND GIVES

2 HER A KISS.) Thank you for being my

3 friend. (DEENA EXITS.)

4                    RAY

5 You know, you're a pretty special

6 lady.

7                    JANA

8 Stop it, Ray. You're embarrassing me.

9                    RAY

10 It's true. You have such a good

11 spirit. I'll bet you have never told

12 a lie in your entire life.

13 (CLOSE ON JANA.)

14 FADE TO BLACK

1                    *ACT 4 SCENE 1*

2 (PAM'S APARTMENT. DAY. STEVE AND

3 KAREN ARE ON THE COUCH.)

4                         STEVE

5 Would you like another daiquiri?

6                         KAREN

7 Oh, no, thanks. I have to work

8 tonight. I really can't believe I got

9 the job. It seems like such a fun

10 place to work. Everyone seems so

11 friendly.

12                        STEVE

13 Sure you wouldn't like another drink?

14                        KAREN

15 These really are good. It'd be great

16 to be able to make so many exotic

17 drinks.

18

1                    STEVE

2 Exotic and erotic. They always seem

3 to make people mellow out.

4                    KAREN

5 I guess I must seem like a nervous

6 wreck. I'm just so excited about

7 working at the Boar's Head.

8                    STEVE

9 It's the kind of place where you can

10 let your hair down and cut loose. (HE

11 SLOWLY PULLS THE CLIP OUT OF HER HAIR

12 AND LETS IT FALL.)

13                   KAREN

14 (BECOMING A LITTLE UNEASY.) I

15 appreciate your inviting me over. I

16 have a thousand questions to ask you.

17 (SHE MOVES AWAY FROM HIM.)

1              STEVE

2 I have a couple I want to ask you.

3              KAREN

4 Al is so sweet, isn't he? I'm gonna

5 enjoy working for him.

6              STEVE

7 But, I'll be your immediate boss.

8 Like the captain of the ship. Total

9 disciplinary control.

10             KAREN

11 (TRYING TO LAUGH IT OFF.) You don't

12 have to worry about me. I'll show up

13 on time and I won't cause any

14 trouble.

15             STEVE

16 Yeah, trouble. That's my middle name.

17             KAREN

18 (SHE IGNORES THAT STATEMENT.) I just

19 want to make a good impression. I was

1 so happy when Al hired me. Right on

2 the spot. It was the first place I've

3 applied to since I got ... you know,

4 fired.

5                    STEVE

6 I'm surprised they let you go. If I

7 had you, I'd hold you so tight you

8 would never get away. (HE GIVES HER A

9 BIG SMILE.)

10                    KAREN

11 You're sweet. I was going to try my

12 hand at being a waitress, but all my

13 friends said that tips are better as

14 a cocktail waitress. You think I'll

15 make good tips?

16

1                    STEVE

2  (MOVING CLOSER TO HER.) With a face

3  and body like yours? You won't have

4  any problem making good tips.

5                    KAREN

6  Thanks. I'm gonna be the best

7  waitress they ever had. (HE BEGINS TO

8  MOVE IN CLOSER TO HER. SHE IS

9  BEGINNING TO FEEL UNCOMFORTABLE.)

10                   STEVE

11 I'm countin' on that. (JUST AS HE

12 STARTS TO TOUCH HER PAM ENTERS THE

13 ROOM.)

14                   PAM

15 Steven, what are you doing?

16                   KAREN

17 Pam! I didn't know. I mean, we

18 weren't doing anything. I just came

19 by to ... well ... you know ... I'm

1 so embarrassed. I didn't realize that

2 you two ... I ...

3                    PAM

4 What are you talking about, Karen?

5                    KAREN

6 That you ... that you and Steve

7 were ... seeing each other.

8                    PAM

9 Well, now you know. Perhaps you

10 should leave.

11                    STEVE

12 Karen's my friend.

13                    KAREN

14 I really have to go. I didn't

15 mean ...

16                    PAM

17 Karen, don't worry about it. Just

18 leave us alone.

1                    STEVE

2 Come on Karen, I'll walk you out.

3                    KAREN

4 No, really ... that's alright. I'll

5 see ya' later. I'm really sorry, Pam.

6 (SHE EXITS.)

7                    PAM

8 (GOES OVER AN SLAPS HIS FACE.) What

9 the hell do you think that you're

10 doing.

11                   STEVE

12 Gettin' outta here. (HE STORMS OUT

13 THE DOOR.)

14                   PAM

15 (CALLING AFTER HIM.) Steve! Steve,

16 come back here.

17 CUT TO:

18

1                    *ACT 4 SCENE 2*

2 (COFFEE SHOP. MALCOLM IS SITTING AT A

3 TABLE HAVING BREAKFAST. ED ENTERS. HE

4 SEES MALCOLM AND GOES OVER TO HIS

5 TABLE.)

6                      MALCOLM

7 Hello, mate. Would you like to join

8 me for a cup of coffee?

9                        ED

10 We've been looking everywhere for

11 you.

12                     MALCOLM

13 I was out photographing the lake. Why

14 are you looking for me?

15                        ED

16 It's Damon. He's been in an accident.

17                     MALCOLM

18 Oh, no. What happened?

1     ED

2 He was hit by a car late last night.

3 He's in very serious condition.

4     MALCOLM

5 This is all my fault. I should never

6 have left him alone.

7     ED

8 There's no time for that right now.

9 Natalie sent me to look for you. She

10 said that you had to get to the

11 hospital as quickly as possible.

12     MALCOLM

13 Of course. But why does she want me

14 there?

15     ED

16 I really don't know. We just have to

17 get there right away.

18     MALCOLM

19 How bad is it?

1                    ED

2 I just hope we're not too late.

3 CUT TO:

4                    *ACT 4 SCENE 3*

5 (HOSPITAL WAITING ROOM. DAY. NATALIE

6 IS PACING IN THE WAITING AREA. KEVIN

7 COMES INTO THE ROOM.)

8                 NATALIE

9 Well, did you find him?

10                KEVIN

11 I tried. I even went to his hotel

12 room. He wasn't there.

13                NATALIE

14 We have to find him.

15                KEVIN

16 I called Ed and he's trying to track

17 him down.

18

1                    NATALIE

2 I can't believe this is happening.

3 What am I going to say to him? How

4 can I explain it? (DAYNA AND SONJA

5 ENTER.)

6                    DAYNA

7 My God, Natalie, what is going on?

8                    NATALIE

9 Oh, Dayna. Thank you for coming.

10                   SONJA

11 How is he?

12                   NATALIE

13 We don't really know. He's been in

14 and out of surgery. (SHE STARTS TO

15 CRY.) They don't know if he is going

16 to make it.

17                   DAYNA

18 Of, course he's going to make it.

19 He's young and strong.

1                    SONJA

2 I want to know what happened.

3                    KEVIN

4 We don't really know. He was hit by a

5 car.

6                    DAYNA

7 What?

8                    KEVIN

9 He was hit by a car near the docks.

10                   SONJA

11 What in the world was he doing down

12 there?

13                   NATALIE

14 We don't know. Whoever hit him didn't

15 even stop.

16                   DAYNA

17 What do the doctors say?

18

1              KEVIN

2 He's suffered head and spinal

3 injuries.

4              NATALIE

5 They don't know if he'll ever be able

6 to walk again. (SHE BEGINS CRYING

7 AGAIN.)

8              SONJA

9 It's all my fault. If I hadn't broken

10 up with him this would never have

11 happened. (WES ENTERS.)

12              NATALIE

13 What's going on?

14              WES

15 It is extremely critical. We need the

16 blood and we need it now. (KEVIN

17 LOOKS AT NATALIE.)

18 (CLOSE ON NATALIE.)

19 CUT TO:

1               *ACT 5 SCENE 1*

2 (PAM'S APARTMENT. NIGHT. STEVE

3 ENTERS. IT IS DARK AND QUIET. HE

4 THINKS HE IS ALONE. HE CROSSES TO

5 COUCH AND SITS TO RELAX. PAM ENTERS

6 AND TURNS ON THE LIGHTS.)

7               PAM

8 So, you finally decided to come home.

9               STEVE

10 Well, if it bothers you I'll leave.

11 (HE STARTS TO GET UP. PAM PUSHES HIM

12 DOWN ON THE COUCH.)

13               PAM

14 (SHAKING HIM.) You're not going

15 anywhere.

16               STEVE

17 I didn't do anything.

18

1                   PAM

2 And I'm going to make sure you don't.

3 How could you ever think of bringing

4 someone into my apartment?

5                   STEVE

6 It wasn't my fault.

7                   PAM

8 It never is. (BEAT.) Alright ...

9 alright. Look, Steve. I'm willing to

10 forget this ever happened if you will

11 promise me not to bring anyone home

12 again.

13                  STEVE

14 Alright.

15                  PAM

16 And you mustn't see Karen again

17 either.

18                  STEVE

19 Alright.

1            PAM

2 I can't afford for anyone to find out

3 anything personal about me. Listen

4 Steve, I'm going to tell you a

5 secret, if you promise not to tell

6 anyone.

7            STEVE

8 I promise.

9            PAM

10 I'm working at B&R, but I'm getting

11 paid a lot more by someone else to

12 pass on important information.

13            STEVE

14 You're a corporate spy?

15            PAM

16 That's right, Steve. So, now you see

17 how important it is for me that no

18 one asks questions. I have built up a

1 life here. No family; no connections;

2 no questions. Okay?

3                    STEVE

4 I'm sorry Pam. I would never do

5 anything to hurt you.

6                    PAM

7 I know you wouldn't, Steve. But,

8 sometimes you don't think about what

9 you do.

10                   STEVE

11 I know. I'm sorry. You're the only

12 family I have.

13                   PAM

14 You'll always have me. So, if

15 anyone ... anyone at all, asks you

16 any questions, don't say anything.

17                   STEVE

18 Okay.

19

1           PAM

2 Come on. I'll get your pillow and

3 blanket. (PAM EXITS.)

4 CUT TO:

5           *ACT 5 SCENE 2*

6 (HOSPITAL WAITING ROOM. NATALIE AND

7 DAYNA ARE SITTING TOGETHER AT A

8 TABLE. SONJA AND KEVIN ARE TALKING IN

9 THE CORNER. MALCOLM ENTERS WITH ED.

10 NATALIE RUNS OVER TO MALCOLM.)

11           NATALIE

12 What's your blood type?

13           MALCOLM

14 My blood type?

15           NATALIE

16 Yes, what is it?

17           MALCOLM

18 AB negative. Why?

1                    NATALIE

2 Kevin, get the doctor.

3                    MALCOLM

4 What is going on? What is this about

5 my blood type?

6                    NATALIE

7 Damon has to have a transfusion. Now!

8 If not he's going to die.

9                    MALCOLM

10 Damon has my blood type?

11                   KEVIN

12 There is no time for conversation.

13 Come with me. (MALCOLM STARES AT

14 NATALIE FOR A SECOND AND THEN FOLLOWS

15 KEVIN. ED WALKS OVER TO HER.)

16                   NATALIE

17 You didn't tell him.

18

```
1                    ED

2 I didn't think that it was my place

3 to tell him.

4                 NATALIE

5 You're right. I'll have to do it.

6                    ED

7 He did tell me something.

8                 NATALIE

9 What?

10                   ED

11 He was with Damon last night.

12                NATALIE

13 What do you mean he was with Damon?

14                   ED

15 They were out drinking together.

16
```

1                    NATALIE

2 Drinking? What are you talking about?

3 Damon is too young to drink. Doesn't

4 Malcolm know that?

5                      ED

6 Yes. And he feels terrible about it.

7 He tried to get Damon to go home, but

8 he wouldn't. So, he took his car

9 keys.

10                   NATALIE

11 He left Damon by himself. Drunk.

12                     ED

13 Natalie, he feels terrible about it.

14                   NATALIE

15 I can't believe he did this.

16                     ED

17 Well, it's done. Right now you'd

18 better come up with a reason for not

1 telling him that Damon is his son.

2 (CLOSE ON NATALIE.)

3 CUT TO:

4                    *ACT 5 SCENE 3*

5 (JAMES' LIVING ROOM. NIGHT. SHANNON

6 IS SITTING ON THE SOFA READING. THERE

7 IS A KNOCK ON THE DOOR.)

8                    SHANNON

9 I'll get it, Helga. (SHE GOES TO THE

10 DOOR.) I'm sorry. It's very late.

11                    TERESA

12 Please, Shannon. Let me in. I need to

13 talk to you.

14                    SHANNON

15 There is nothing to talk about.

16

```
1               TERESA

2  Shannon, please. I haven't been

3  drinking. Let me speak to you.

4  (SHANNON LETS HER IN.)

5               SHANNON

6  Would you care for some coffee?

7               TERESA

8  No, thank you. Tell me ... tell me

9  where Greg is?

10              SHANNON

11 I swear, Mrs. Reed. I don't know.

12              TERESA

13 I have to know. Is he alright?

14              SHANNON

15 Mrs. Reed, I haven't heard from him.

16              TERESA

17 (SHE TRIES TO CONTROL HER TEMPER)

18 Please, don't lie to me Shannon. I

19 know that you know where he is.
```

1               SHANNON

2 I think you'd better leave now.

3                TERESA

4 Please, Shannon. I'm sorry. Please

5 help me.

6               SHANNON

7 I didn't lie to you. I don't know

8 where he is.

9                TERESA

10 Why didn't he come to me?

11               SHANNON

12 Because you wouldn't understand.

13                TERESA

14 How could I not understand? I'm his

15 mother.

16               SHANNON

17 That's probably why you wouldn't

18 understand.

1                    TERESA

2 It's drugs, isn't it?

3                    SHANNON

4 Yes, there are some people

5 threatening him.

6                    TERESA

7 Oh, my God. I knew it all along. I

8 should have gotten him treatment.

9                    SHANNON

10 Didn't you hear me? His life is in

11 danger.

12                    TERESA

13 We could have gone to the police. I

14 could have helped him.

15                    SHANNON

16 That's right. Call the police. Have

17 him put away. All you would do is

18 humiliate him.

19

1                    TERESA

2 He needs me.

3                    SHANNON

4 If you had been there when he needed

5 you, he wouldn't be in trouble now.

6                    TERESA

7 (THEY ARE SHOUTING NOW.) Why would

8 you say that to me? I have always

9 loved him. (TRES ENTERS AND STANDS IN

10 THE DOORWAY.)

11                    SHANNON

12 (UNABLE TO CONTROL HER ANGER.) Maybe

13 if you had let him know that he

14 wouldn't have run away. You parents

15 are all the same. You talk about

16 love, but you never talk about

17 respect. You just don't give a damn.

18 (SHE RUNS OUT OF THE ROOM.)

```
1                    TERESA

2 (TURNING TO TRES.) How could she say

3 these things to me?

4                    TRES

5 She's upset. She didn't mean it.

6                    TERESA

7 She should at least tell me where he

8 is.

9                    TRES

10 Mrs. Reed, she doesn't know where he

11 is. She's worried sick about him.

12                   TERESA

13 I'm sorry. I'm just so frightened.

14                   TRES

15 (GOES OVER AND PUTS HIS ARMS AROUND

16 HER.) I know. (SHE STARTS TO EXIT.)

17                   TERESA

18 (SHE TURNS BACK.) I'm sorry about

19 last night.
```

```
1                    TRES

2 Forget it. It's alright.

3                    TERESA

4 I know I shouldn't drink. I can't.

5 You were so kind to me.

6                    TRES

7 You really don't have to say

8 anything.

9                    TERESA

10 I'm sorry if I hurt you.

11                   TRES

12 I don't know what you are talking

13 about.

14                   TERESA

15 It's alright. I understand. (SHE

16 TURNS AND WALKS AWAY.)

17 CUT TO:

18
```

1               ACT 6

2 (PAM'S APARTMENT. LATE NIGHT. STEVE

3 IS ON THE SOFA, TOSSING, TURNING AND

4 TALKING IN HIS SLEEP. HIS AGITATION

5 BUILDS.)

6               STEVE

7 No ... I won't ... I won't tell ... I

8 promise ... Don't ... Please don't

9 hurt me ... Please ... Stop ... (HE

10 IS NOW VERY LOUD.) STOP ... NO!!!!

11              PAM

12 (SWITCHING ON THE LIGHTS. SHE RUNS

13 INTO THE ROOM GOING OVER TO STEVE.)

14 Steve ... Steven ... (SHE SHAKES HIM

15 AS HE STILL STRUGGLES TO WAKE. HE IS

16 STILL SCREAMING.)  Stevie ... (SHE

17 SHAKES HIM MORE.) Honey, snap out of

18 it. Steve. (HE OPENS HIS EYES.)

19

1               STEVE

2 Mama ... Mama ... Don't let them hurt

3 me.

4               PAM

5 (WIPING HIS FACE.) Oh God, Stevie ...

6 Stevie, baby.

7               STEVE

8 (LOOKING AT PAM.) Mama? Is that you

9 Mama?

10              PAM

11 (SHE BEGINS TO CRY.) Yes, darling.

12 Mama's here. You're gonna be okay,

13 baby. (TEARS POUR DOWN HER FACE.)

14 Mama will take care of you.

15              STEVE

16 It hurts, Mama. It hurts.

17

1                    PAM

2 I know honey. I know. Let me get you

3 some milk.

4                    STEVE

5 No, Mama. No! Don't leave me. Don't

6 leave me alone. It's dark. Don't

7 leave me alone.

8                    PAM

9 I won't honey. Mama won't leave you.

10                   STEVE

11 I didn't mean to do it Mama.

12                   PAM

13 I know, honey. I know you didn't.

14                   STEVE

15 They make me so angry.

16                   PAM

17 Who does? Who makes you so angry?

18

1                    STEVE

2 They all do. I don't want to do it,

3 but they make me.

4                    PAM

5 It's all right, Stevie. I won't let

6 them do it. (STEVE IS BECOMING MORE

7 AND MORE CALM AS PAM ROCKS HIM IN HER

8 ARMS, AND SINGS.) Hush little baby,

9 don't say a word, Mama's gonna buy

10 you a mocking bird. And if that

11 mocking bird don't sing, Mama's gonna

12 buy you a diamond ring. (PAM IS

13 CRYING PROFUSELY.)

14 FREEZE FRAME / ROLE CREDITS

15 FADE TO BLACK.

# WORKBOOK
# TUTOR

*CONFIDENCE & CLARITY:*

*The Complete Guide to
Instant Line-Learning*

1                    *ACT 1 SCENE 1*

2 (POLICE HOLDING ROOM. DAY.)

3                    DON

4 Have you lost your mind? If you think

5 that you're going to blackmail me

6 into ...

7                    CAROLYN

8 I have no intention of blackmailing

9 you into anything. You got me into

10 this mess, and if you think that I'm

11 going to keep quiet about it you're

12 wrong.

13                    DON

14 One thing has nothing to do with the

15 other. The police have no knowledge

16 of our little adventure. Whatever

17 they have on you concerning Kathleen

18 has nothing to do with me.

1                    CAROLYN

2 There's where you're wrong. It has

3 everything to do with you.

4                DON

5 Carolyn, I know that you're

6 frightened about all this ...
——— END OF 1ST THIRD

7                CAROLYN

8 Frightened? That's the understatement

9 of the year. I'm terrified! I'm

10 accused of killing someone. I didn't

11 do it.

12                DON

13 If that's true, then you have nothing

14 to fear.

15                CAROLYN

16 Oh, that's easy for you to say, Don.

17 You're not the one accused of murder.

18

1                           DON

2 You don't even know what the police

3 have against you. You'd be better off

4 keeping your mouth shut and waiting

5 to find out what evidence they have.

6                          CAROLYN

7 I know what evidence they have. They

8 know that I brought her to St.

9 Michaels. They know that I gave her a

10 phony resume.  And, they know that I

11 have a police record.

——————— *END OF 2ND THIRD*

12                           DON

13 One thing has nothing to do with the

14 other.

15                         CAROLYN

16 They seem to think that it does.

17 Kathleen was killed as a warning. I

18 know it, and so do you.

1                DON

2 I don't know anything of the kind.

3 You're gonna make a big mistake if

4 you don't start getting control of

5 yourself. Now, for once in your life,

6 listen. Everything they have against

7 you is circumstantial. There is

8 nothing that will hold up in a court

9 of law. They're trying to get you

10 spooked -- trying to make you

11 confess.

12              CAROLYN

13 I will not confess to something that

14 I didn't do. Whoever killed her is

15 setting me up. Well, they won't get

16 away with it.

17              DON

18 You'd better listen to me, Carolyn.

19 Keep your mouth shut. Wait 'til all

1 the facts are in, and then you'll

2 have a chance of dealing with your

3 defense. If you don't, you're gonna

4 hang yourself. (DETECTIVE WILSON

5 ENTERS.)

F.S.

6                        DETECTIVE WILSON

7 Who gave you permission to see Ms.

8 Vallacie?

9                        CAROLYN

10 Stop calling me that. My name is

11 Carolyn Costa.

12                        DETECTIVE WILSON

13 Call yourself what you want.

14 "Vallacie" is what we have on your

15 police files and that is what it's

16 going to be. I want to know what

17 you're doing here, Don?

END OF 1ST THIRD

18

1               DON

2 Carolyn is an acquaintance of mine.

3 She called me for advice.

4               DETECTIVE WILSON

5 Are you her attorney?

6               DON

7 No, I am not.

8               DETECTIVE WILSON

9 Then, I'll have to ask you to leave.
——————— *END OF 2ND THIRD*

10              CAROLYN

11 Wait one minute ...

12              DON

13 That's alright, Carolyn. I'll speak

14 to the District Attorney about this.

15 (TO DON.) If you'll excuse me.

16              CAROLYN

17 Don, wait ...

18

1                    DON

2 Don't worry, Carolyn. You'll be just

3 fine. I'll talk with you later. (HE

4 EXITS.)
              ——— F. S.

5                    CAROLYN

6 You are very rude, Sergeant.

7                  DETECTIVE WILSON

8 It's "Detective", and I'm sorry you

9 feel that way.

10                    CAROLYN

11 When am I getting out of here?
       ——— END OF 1ST THIRD
12                  DETECTIVE WILSON

13 Not any time soon. I'll get the

14 matron to take you back to your cell.

15                    CAROLYN

16 Detective, wait ...

17                  DETECTIVE WILSON

18 Yeah?
       ——— END OF 2ND THIRD

1               CAROLYN

2 (PUTTING ON HER CHARM.) I didn't do

3 it. You must believe me. I'm

4 innocent. I'll do anything to prove

5 that to you. Anything.

6               DON

7 Nice try, Ms. Vallacie. The only

8 person you have to prove it to is the

9 judge. Have a nice day. (HE EXITS.
————— F.S. (NO DIALOGUE F.S.)
10 CAROLYN IS LEFT THWARTED, YET AGAIN.)
————— F.S.
11 CUT TO:

12               *ACT 1 SCENE 2*

13 (JANA'S APARTMENT. DAY.)

14               DEENA

15 Why did you call me "Deena"?

16               JANA

17 Stop it, Deena. I don't know what

18 you're trying to do, but it won't

19 work.

1                    DEENA

2 I'm not trying to do anything.

3                    JANA

4 You're just digging a hole that

5 you're never gonna get out of. Stop

6 it, while there's still time.

7                    DEENA

8 I'm Ruth. My name is Ruth.

9                    JANA

10 Your name is Deena. Deena Murphy. I

11 know it and so do you. I want to help

12 you, but I can't if you continue to

13 lie.

14                    DEENA

15 (BREAKING INTO TEARS.) What am I

16 gonna do? Please help me.

—— END OF 1ˢᵗ THIRD

17

1               JANA

2 Calm down. Now, let's just talk about

3 this. It's too late to worry about

4 what you've done. We have to figure a

5 way to get you out of this.

6               DEENA

7 I'll just say my memory came back.

8               JANA

9 You can't use a lie to replace a lie.

10 That's just gonna cause more trouble.

11              DEENA

12 How did you know?

13              JANA

14 Yesterday, when Dean was here, I

15 knew.

16              DEENA

17 I don't understand.
——— END OF 2ND THIRD

18

1                    JANA

2 It was in your voice ... your eyes.

3 You knew how much you were hurting

4 him. Ruth could never have known.

5                    DEENA

6 I'm such a fool. Why did I want to

7 hurt him like this? I love him Jana,

8 I really do. I'm so sorry. Oh God,

9 I'm sorry.

10                   JANA

11 So, now what? What do you want to do?

12                   DEENA

13 I know exactly what I'm gonna do.

14 (SHE GETS UP AND STARTS TO HEAD FOR

15 HER ROOM.)

16                   JANA

17 Where are you going?

18

1                    DEENA

2 To get dressed. I've got to make it

3 right. (DEENA EXITS.)

4 CUT TO: F.S.

5                    *ACT 1 SCENE 3*

6 (HOSPITAL WAITING ROOM.)

7                    NATALIE

8 You're frightening me. Oh God, he's

9 not ... Please he's not ...

10                   WES

11 No. He's not dead. But, he has

12 suffered traumatic injuries.

13                   NATALIE

14 What kind of injuries?

15                   WES

16 He's suffered major head and spinal

17 injuries.

18

1                    NATALIE

2 Oh, my God. Does this mean he's going

3 to be crippled?

4                    WES

5 It's too soon to tell. We still have

6 tests to run. My immediate concern,

7 however, is his loss of blood.

*—— END OF 1ˢᵗ THIRD*

8                    KEVIN

9 What about transfusions?

10                    WES

11 Unfortunately, it's not that simple.

12 Damon is AB negative.

13                    NATALIE

14 AB negative? What does that mean?

15                    WES

16 It means it's extremely rare. We were

17 able to have one pint transferred

18 from Chicago General.

1           KEVIN

2 Surely, Chicago General has more than

3 one pint of AB negative.

*END OF 2ND THIRD*

4           WES

5 As I said, it's extremely rare. We

6 have a call out for donors, but we

7 really haven't got any time.

8           NATALIE

9 Well, isn't there someone in St.

10 Michaels with that blood type?

11           WES

12 Not on record. If his parents were

13 alive, at least one of them would

14 have to have AB negative. But, as his

15 records show, both his parents are

16 deceased.

17           NATALIE

18 Can I see him?

19

1                    WES

2 I'm sorry, Miss Gardner. That's

3 impossible. Excuse me. (EXITS)
   —— F.S.

4                  NATALIE

5 Kevin, I don't have AB negative.

6                   KEVIN

7 So, Malcolm must.

8 (CLOSE ON NATALIE.)

9 FADE TO BLACK
   —— F.S.

*DON'T BREAK UP*

10              *ACT 2 SCENE 1*

11 (DON'S APARTMENT. DAY. DEAN COMES

12 DOWN THE STAIRS INTO THE LIVING ROOM.
   —— F.S. — No DIALOGUE

13 ROBERT ENTERS FROM STAGE RIGHT

14 CARRYING AN ARRANGEMENT OF FLOWERS.)

15                   DEAN

16 Is Don home?

17                 ROBERT

18 No.  END OT 1ˢᵀ THIRD

1                    DEAN

2 Do you know where he is?

3                    ROBERT

4 He went out early this morning. He

5 didn't say when he would be home.

6 Would you like some lunch?
       —— END OF 2ND THIRD

7                    DEAN

8 No thank you. I've got to get to

9 class. I'll have something at the

10 cafeteria. (DON ENTERS.)
       —— F.S.

11                   ROBERT

12 Good morning, sir. Would you care for

13 lunch?

14                   DON

15 No thank you, Robert. I'll call you

16 if I need anything.

17                   ROBERT

18 Very well, sir. (ROBERT EXITS.)
       —— F.S.

19

DON'T BREAK UP

1              DON

2 What happened to you last night,

3 Dean?

4              DEAN

5 What do you mean?

6              DON

7 You came home and went directly to

8 your room without a word.

9              DEAN

10 Oh ... I was just upset about

11 something.

12              DON

13 Anything you want to share?

14              DEAN

15 It's no big deal.

16              DON

17 Dean, I brought you into my home. If

18 you're having a problem, I need to

1 know what it is. (DEAN HESITATES.)

2 Well, what is it?

3                    DEAN

4 I went to see Deena.

5                    DON

6 You what?

7                    DEAN

8 I had to, Don. I love her and I need

9 her to know it.

10                   DON

11 And ...  *END OF 1ˢᵗ THIRD*

12                   DEAN

13 When she didn't recognize me, I

14 pretended that I didn't know her.

15                   DON

16 Oh, Dean ...

17                   DEAN

18 I had to. I was afraid she'd hate me.

19

1               DON

2 And what happened?

3               DEAN

4 We got along great. She even took me

5 to the country club to help me get a

6 job as a bartender.

7               DON

8 Dean, are you crazy? You expected to

9 go back to the place where Deena was

10 hurt to get a job? What in the world

11 were you thinking?

12              DEAN

13 I know. It was stupid.  And I mean

14 really stupid.

15              DON

16 What are you saying Dean?

17

1           DEAN

2 Deena's aunt was there and she ...

3 she ...

4           DON

5 She what!?!?

6           DEAN

7 She hit me.
          ——— END OF 2ND THIRD
8           DON

9 Dean, I can't believe this. Do you

10 realize that this whole thing could

11 blow up in your face?

12          DEAN

13 I didn't mean to ...

14          DON

15 It doesn't matter what you meant. The

16 damage is done. You have to swear to

17 me you will not go near her again.

18          DEAN

19 I can't do that.

1                       DON

2 You not only can, but you will. Until

3 the charges have been dropped against

4 you, you will not see her again.

5                       DEAN

6 I already have.

7                       DON

8 When?

9                       DEAN

10 Yesterday. I had to tell her

11 about ...

12                       DON

13 About what?

14                       DEAN

15 I can't.

16                       DON

17 Tell her about what?!?!

18

1                    DEAN

2  (BEAT.) Our child, damn it.  Our

3  child. *(Eventhough this dialogue*

*continues in Act 2 Scene 2,*

*a script break creates a*

4  (CLOSE OUT ON DON.) *French Scene.)*

5  CUT TO:
        ——— *F.S.*

6                *ACT 2 SCENE 2*

7  (DAYNA'S BEDROOM. MORNING. DAYNA HAS

8  HER HEAD COVERED UNDER THE SHEET.
        ——— *F.S.*

9  SONJA ENTERS.)

10                   SONJA

11 Mother? Mother. Are you going to get

12 up?

13                   DAYNA

14 Leave me alone.

15                   SONJA

16 (PULLING THE COVERS AWAY FROM HER

17 HEAD.) Mother, this is silly.

18                   DAYNA

19 Just leave me alone.

1                    SONJA

2 (PICKS UP A BOTTLE OF SLEEPING PILLS

3 SITTING BESIDE THE BED.) Oh, my God!

4 How many of these did you take?

5                    DAYNA

6 (LOOKING AROUND TO SEE WHAT SHE IS

7 TALKING ABOUT.) One. (SHE TAKES THE

8 COVERS AND PULLS THEM BACK OVER HER

9 HEAD.) *END OF 1ˢᵀ THIRD*

10                   SONJA

11 Are you doing this because of Martin?

12 (DAYNA BURIES HERSELF DEEPER UNDER

13 THE COVERS.) Mother, Martin has his

14 own life to lead. He'll come to his

15 senses. Let him do what he has to do.

16                   DAYNA

17 I don't want to talk about it. Just

18 get out of here.

1                    SONJA

2 I am not getting out of here. (SHE

3 PULLS THE COVERS BACK.) Now, I want

4 you to get up and pull yourself

5 together. You have things to do.

6                    DAYNA

7 Let someone else do them. Martin has

8 ruined all my plans.

9                    SONJA

10 What plans?

11                   DAYNA

12 (TRYING TO GET THE COVERS FROM

13 SONJA.) It doesn't matter anymore.

——— END OF 2ND THIRD

14                   SONJA

15 Of course, it matters. Talk to me.

16 What plans has Martin ruined?

17                   DAYNA

18 (SITTING UP IN BED.) I wanted Martin

19 to find a nice wife and you a

1 wonderful husband. Then you would all

2 start raising families right here in

3 St. Michaels. I wanted us to have a

4 real family that celebrated birthdays

5 and holidays. I just wanted ... (SHE

6 BEGINS TO CRY.)

7                    SONJA

8 Oh, Mother. (TAKING DAYNA IN HER

9 ARMS.) I'm sorry. Please, don't cry.

10 Maybe it will still happen. Maybe

11 he'll come home and ...

12                    DAYNA

13 No, he won't. He's gone. I know he

14 is. He'll find that woman and marry

15 her and I'll never see him again.

16                    SONJA

17 You're making too much out of this.

18 He'll be back. I know he will. (THE

1 PHONE RINGS. SONJA GOES PICKS IT UP.)

2 Yes, Alice. ⌐ F. S. (PAUSE.) Just tell

3 whoever it is that Mother will call

4 them back. (PAUSE.) What! Oh, my

5 God ...

6                     DAYNA

7 (SITTING UP QUICKLY IN BED.) It's

8 Martin. Something has happened to

9 Martin.

10                     SONJA

11 (TRYING TO HUSH HER MOTHER AS SHE

12 FINISHES LISTENING TO THE

13 CONVERSATION.) Yes, thank you. (SHE

14 HANGS UP THE PHONE.)
                ────── F. S.
15                     DAYNA

16 What? Tell me!

17                     SONJA

18 It's Damon. He's been seriously

19 injured in an accident.

1              DAYNA

2 Oh, no! (SHE GRABS HER ROBE AS SHE

3 GETS OUT OF BED.) Where is he?

4              SONJA

5 He's having emergency surgery. (SHE

6 GRABS HER HEAD IN PAIN.)

—— END OF 1ST THIRD

7              DAYNA

8 I know he'll be alright. (SHE TRIES

9 TO COMFORT SONJA.) Get hold of

10 yourself. Come on, I have to get

11 dressed and we'll go to the hospital.

12              SONJA

13 Why? I don't want to go to the

14 hospital.

15              DAYNA

16 We have to go see about Damon. What

17 is wrong with you?

—— END OF 2ND THIRD

18

1               SONJA

2 There is nothing wrong with me. If

3 you want to go to the hospital then

4 go but ... Oh! (SHE GRABS HER HEAD

5 AGAIN.)

6               DAYNA

7 Sonja, are you alright? (SHE DOES NOT

8 RESPOND.) Sonja, answer me.

9               SONJA

10 Hurry up. We have to get to the

11 hospital.

12 (CLOSE ON DAYNA.)

13 FADE TO BLACK
       F.S.

14               *ACT 2 SCENE 3*

15 (DON'S APARTMENT. DON AND DEAN ARE

16 STILL ARGUING.)

17               DON

18 I can't believe that you and Deena

19 had a child.

1                    DEAN

2 But, she gave it up for adoption. I

3 didn't know. I want my child back. I

4 want them both back. I want us to be

5 a family.

6                    DON

7 Were you married?

8                    DEAN

9 No.

10                    DON

11 Listen, Dean. You're setting yourself

12 up for a terrible fall.

—— *END OF 1ˢᵗ THIRD*

13                    DEAN

14 No!

15                    DON

16 Yes, you are. You have no legal right

17 to that child.

18

1                    DEAN

2 But, I'm the father.

3                    DON

4 I know how you must feel. But,

5 please, forget about this. There is

6 nothing that you can do about it.
— END OF 2ND THIRD

7                    DEAN

8 I can't forget about it. I can't!

9                    DON

10 Dean, I promise I'll do anything that

11 I can to help you. But you are going

12 to have to accept certain truths.

13                    DEAN

14 I don't have to accept anything. It's

15 my child. Nobody asked me. I have

16 rights, too.

17                    DON

18 You're not going to get anywhere

19 until you learn to calm down. We'll

ROBERT

1 think of something. Try to get

2 control of your feelings and deal

3 with this in a rational manner.

4 (ROBERT ENTERS.)
—— F. S.
5         ROBERT

6 Excuse me, Mr. Croft. Your lawyer is

7 here to see you.

8         DON

9 Thank you, Robert. Give me a minute

10 and then send him in. (ROBERT EXITS.)
—— F. S.
11         DEAN

12 I have to get to class. (HE STARTS TO

13 EXIT.)

14         DON

15 Dean.

16         DEAN

17 Yes?

18

1               DON

2 Don't do anything irrational. We'll

3 figure something out. Alright?

4               DEAN
                    ⌐ F.S.
5 Sure. (HE EXITS.⌐DON WATCHES HIM

6 LEAVE. ROBERT ENTERS WITH MARK.)
        — F.S.
7               DON

8 Hello, Mark. I wasn't expecting you

9 this morning.

10              MARK

11 Sorry I didn't call first. I have a

12 few things that we need to discuss.

13              DON

14 What is it?

15              ROBERT

16 Would you care for something before I

17 leave?

18

1                DON
                      F.S.⌐
2 No, nothing. (ROBERT EXITS.) Well,

3 what is it?

4                MARK

5 (HE OPENS HIS BRIEFCASE AND TAKES OUT

6 A FOLDER.) I need you to sign these

7 papers.

8                DON

9 (TAKES THE FOLDER.) What are they?

10               MARK

11 Sundae had a special account in

12 Switzerland.

13               DON

14 Sundae had a Swiss account?

15               MARK

16 Yes, she was a shrewd business

17 person. She diversified her

18 inheritance into T-bills, stocks and

1 some dealings that were, shall we

2 say, different.
— *END OF 1ˢᵗ THIRD*

3                          DON

4 (LOOKING AT THE FIGURES.) My word.

5 This is beyond the other monies she

6 had?

7                      MARK

8 Yes.

9                      DON

10 I can't believe this.

11                      MARK

12 Well, it's true. Just sign both sides

13 of the document and then the money

14 can be released. (DON TAKES A PEN

15 FROM HIS JACKET AND BEGINS TO SIGN.)

16 There is one small problem.

17                      DON

18 What kind of small problem?

19

1                    MARK

2 She never claimed the money.
    —— END OF 2^(ND) THIRD
3                    DON

4 Meaning?

5                    MARK

6 Meaning there is going to be quite a

7 large tax fee.

8                    DON

9 Oh. Is there anyway around it?

10                   MARK

11 I'm afraid not. It will eat up about

12 70 percent.

13                   DON

14 Seventy percent?

15                   MARK

16 I wouldn't worry too much. It'll

17 still keep you in pocket change for a

1 few hundred years. (DON SIGNS THE

2 PAPERS.)

3 CUT TO: ─ F.S.

4                    *ACT 3*

5 (JANA'S APARTMENT. RAY AND JANA ARE

6 HAVING LUNCH AT THE KITCHEN COUNTER.)

7                    RAY

8 This is not exactly what I had in

9 mind when I said we should have a

10 Saturday lunch.

11                   JANA

12 I'm Sorry, Ray. I just don't want to

13 leave the house until I know what's

14 going on with Deena.

15                   RAY

16 I was just kidding. I'm having a

17 great time.

18                   JANA

19 Thank you. You want some more pasta?

1                    RAY

2 I've got (pasta) up to my eyeballs.

3 Thanks, anyway.

4                    JANA

5 You didn't like it.

    —— END OF 1ST THIRD

6                    RAY

7 I did like it. I think you're being a

8 little touchy.

9                    JANA

10 (SHE STARTS TO REMOVE THE PLATES.) I

11 know. I really am sorry. It has just

12 been such an unbelievable morning.

13                    RAY

14 Because of Deena?

15                    JANA

16 Yes. I can't tell you what it was

17 like. I've never spoken to anyone

1 like that before. I should have just

2 stayed out of it.

3                    RAY

4 Wrong. You did what you had to do.

5 Stop feeling guilty. She's lucky that

6 she has someone like you to care

7 about her. Not many people would have

8 been as gracious.

—— END OF 2ND THIRD

9                    JANA

10 I just know where she's coming from.

11                    RAY

12 Meaning?

13                    JANA

14 Meaning ... meaning I understand what

15 she's going through. That's all. Now,

16 what would you like for dessert?

17                    RAY

18 You sound pretty good to me. (HE GOES

19 OVER AND PUTS HIS ARMS AROUND HER.)

1                         JANA

2 Very funny. I didn't know that I was

3 on the menu.

4                         RAY

5 Well, now you do. (HE STARTS TO KISS

6 HER WHEN DEENA COMES INTO THE ROOM.)
   —— F.S.
7                         DEENA

8 Oh, I'm sorry.

9                         JANA

10 (TO DEENA.) Forget it. Where did you

11 go? I've been worried about you.

12                        DEENA

13 I went to the police station.

14                        JANA

15 The police station? Whatever for?
   —— END OF 1ST THIRD
16                        DEENA

17 I had to make something right. At

18 least it's a start.

```
1                    JANA

2  What about Natalie?

3                    DEENA

4  I went by her house, but no one was

5  there. I'll call her later. I'm

6  really very tired. If you'll excuse

7  me I want to lie down.
```

—— END OF 2ND THIRD

```
8                    JANA

9  Deena, what you are doing is right. I

10 hope that you know that.

11                   DEENA

12 I know. Now I have to deal with my

13 mother.

14                   JANA

15 Your mother?

16                   DEENA

17 I didn't tell you? She's coming to

18 St. Michaels. I'll talk to you later.

19 (SHE STARTS TO GO TO HER ROOM AND
```

1 THEN STOPS. CROSSES TO JANA AND GIVES

2 HER A KISS.) Thank you for being my

3 friend. (DEENA EXITS.)
—— F. S.

4                    RAY

5 You know, you're a pretty special

6 lady.

7                    JANA

8 Stop it, Ray. You're embarrassing me.

9                    RAY

10 It's true. You have such a good

11 spirit. I'll bet you have never told

12 a lie in your entire life.

13 (CLOSE ON JANA.)

14 FADE TO BLACK
—— F. S.

1               *ACT 4 SCENE 1*

2 (PAM'S APARTMENT. DAY. STEVE AND

3 KAREN ARE ON THE COUCH.)

4                    STEVE

5 Would you like another daiquiri?

6                    KAREN

7 Oh, no, thanks. I have to work

8 tonight. I really can't believe I got

9 the job. It seems like such a fun

10 place to work. Everyone seems so

11 friendly.

12                   STEVE

13 Sure you wouldn't like another drink?

14                   KAREN

15 These really are good. It'd be great

16 to be able to make so many exotic

17 drinks.

18

1           STEVE

2 Exotic and erotic. They always seem

3 to make people mellow out.

4           KAREN

5 I guess I must seem like a nervous

6 wreck. I'm just so excited about

7 working at the Boar's Head.
  — END OF 1ST THIRD
8           STEVE

9 It's the kind of place where you can

10 let your hair down and cut loose. (HE

11 SLOWLY PULLS THE CLIP OUT OF HER HAIR

12 AND LETS IT FALL.)

13           KAREN

14 (BECOMING A LITTLE UNEASY.) I

15 appreciate your inviting me over. I

16 have a thousand questions to ask you.

17 (SHE MOVES AWAY FROM HIM.)

1                     STEVE

2 I have a couple I want to ask you.

3                     KAREN

4 Al is so sweet, isn't he? I'm gonna

5 enjoy working for him.

6                     STEVE

7 But, I'll be your immediate boss.

8 Like the captain of the ship. Total

9 disciplinary control.

10                     KAREN

11 (TRYING TO LAUGH IT OFF.) You don't

12 have to worry about me. I'll show up

13 on time and I won't cause any

14 trouble.

15                     STEVE

16 Yeah, trouble. That's my middle name.
——— END OF 2ND THIRD

17                     KAREN

18 (SHE IGNORES THAT STATEMENT.) I just

19 want to make a good impression. I was

1 so happy when Al hired me. Right on

2 the spot. It was the first place I've

3 applied to since I got ... you know,

4 fired.

5                    STEVE

6 I'm surprised they let you go. If I

7 had you, I'd hold you so tight you

8 would never get away. (HE GIVES HER A

9 BIG SMILE.)

10                    KAREN

11 You're sweet. I was going to try my

12 hand at being a waitress, but all my

13 friends said that tips are better as

14 a cocktail waitress. You think I'll

15 make good tips?

16

1                STEVE

2 (MOVING CLOSER TO HER.) With a face

3 and body like yours? You won't have

4 any problem making good tips.

5                KAREN

6 Thanks. I'm gonna be the best

7 waitress they ever had. (HE BEGINS TO

8 MOVE IN CLOSER TO HER. SHE IS

9 BEGINNING TO FEEL UNCOMFORTABLE.)

10                STEVE

11 I'm countin' on that. (JUST AS HE

12 STARTS TO TOUCH HER PAM ENTERS THE

13 ROOM.)
   — F.S.

14                PAM

15 Steven, what are you doing?

16                KAREN

17 Pam! I didn't know. I mean, we

18 weren't doing anything. I just came

19 by to ... well ... you know ... I'm

1 so embarrassed. I didn't realize that

2 you two ... I ...

3                    PAM

4 What are you talking about, Karen?
—— *END OF 1st THIRD*
5                    KAREN

6 That you ... that you and Steve

7 were ... seeing each other.

8                    PAM

9 Well, now you know. Perhaps you

10 should leave.

11                    STEVE

12 Karen's my friend.

13                    KAREN

14 I really have to go. I didn't

15 mean ...
—— *END OF 2ND THIRD*
16                    PAM

17 Karen, don't worry about it. Just

18 leave us alone.

1             STEVE

2 Come on Karen, I'll walk you out.

3             KAREN

4 No, really ... that's alright. I'll

5 see ya' later. I'm really sorry, Pam.

6 (SHE EXITS.)
—— F.S.

7             PAM

8 (GOES OVER AN SLAPS HIS FACE.) What

9 the hell do you think that you're

10 doing.

11             STEVE

12 Gettin' outta here. (HE STORMS OUT

13 THE DOOR.)
—— F.S.

14             PAM

15 (CALLING AFTER HIM.) Steve! Steve,

16 come back here.

17 CUT TO:
—— F.S.

18

1             *ACT 4 SCENE 2*

2 (COFFEE SHOP. MALCOLM IS SITTING AT A

3 TABLE HAVING BREAKFAST. ED ENTERS. F.S. ⌐ HE

4 SEES MALCOLM AND GOES OVER TO HIS

5 TABLE.)

6                   MALCOLM

7 Hello, mate. Would you like to join

8 me for a cup of coffee?

9                   ED

10 We've been looking everywhere for

11 you.

12                  MALCOLM

13 I was out photographing the lake. Why

14 are you looking for me?

15                  ED

16 It's Damon. He's been in an accident.

    ⸺ END OF 1ˢᵀ THIRD

17                  MALCOLM

18 Oh, no. What happened?

1                    ED

2 He was hit by a car late last night.

3 He's in very serious condition.

4                  MALCOLM

5 This is all my fault. I should never

6 have left him alone.

7                    ED

8 There's no time for that right now.

9 Natalie sent me to look for you. She

10 said that you had to get to the

11 hospital as quickly as possible.
   — *END OF 2ND THIRD*

12                 MALCOLM

13 Of course. But why does she want me

14 there?

15                   ED

16 I really don't know. We just have to

17 get there right away.

18                 MALCOLM

19 How bad is it?

1           ED

2 I just hope we're not too late.

3 <u>CUT TO:</u>F.S.

4         *ACT 4 SCENE 3*

5 (HOSPITAL WAITING ROOM. DAY. NATALIE

6 IS PACING IN THE WAITING AREA. KEVIN

7 COMES INTO THE ROOM.)
   — F.S.

8        NATALIE

9 Well, did you find him?

10       KEVIN

11 I tried. I even went to his hotel

12 room. He wasn't there.

13       NATALIE

14 We have to find him.

15       KEVIN

16 I called Ed and he's trying to track

17 him down.

18

1                    NATALIE

2 I can't believe this is happening.

3 What am I going to say to him? How

4 can I explain it? (DAYNA AND SONJA

5 ENTER.)  F.S.

6                    DAYNA

7 My God, Natalie, what is going on?

8                    NATALIE

9 Oh, Dayna. Thank you for coming.

10                   SONJA

11 How is he?

12                   NATALIE

13 We don't really know. He's been in

14 and out of surgery. (SHE STARTS TO

15 CRY.) They don't know if he is going

16 to make it.

17                   DAYNA

18 Of, course he's going to make it.

19 He's young and strong.

— END OF 1ST THIRD

1                     SONJA

2 I want to know what happened.

3                     KEVIN

4 We don't really know. He was hit by a

5 car.

6                     DAYNA

7 What?

8                     KEVIN

9 He was hit by a car near the docks.

10                    SONJA

11 What in the world was he doing down

12 there?

— END OF 2ND THIRD

13                    NATALIE

14 We don't know. Whoever hit him didn't

15 even stop.

16                    DAYNA

17 What do the doctors say?

18

1                    KEVIN

2 He's suffered head and spinal

3 injuries.

4                    NATALIE

5 They don't know if he'll ever be able

6 to walk again. (SHE BEGINS CRYING

7 AGAIN.)

8                    SONJA

9 It's all my fault. If I hadn't broken

10 up with him this would never have

11 happened. (WES ENTERS.)
        —— F.S.

12                   NATALIE

13 What's going on?

14                   WES

15 It is extremely critical. We need the

16 blood and we need it now. (KEVIN

17 LOOKS AT NATALIE.)

18 (CLOSE ON NATALIE.)

19 CUT TO:
        —— F.S.

1               *ACT 5 SCENE 1*

2  (PAM'S APARTMENT. NIGHT. STEVE

⌐ F.S.

3  ENTERS. IT IS DARK AND QUIET. HE

4  THINKS HE IS ALONE. HE CROSSES TO

5  COUCH AND SITS TO RELAX. PAM ENTERS

6  AND TURNS ON THE LIGHTS.)

—— F.S.

7                   PAM

8  So, you finally decided to come home.

9                  STEVE

10  Well, if it bothers you I'll leave.

11  (HE STARTS TO GET UP. PAM PUSHES HIM

12  DOWN ON THE COUCH.)

13                  PAM

14  (SHAKING HIM.) You're not going

15  anywhere.

16                 STEVE

17  I didn't do anything.

18

1              **PAM**

2 And I'm going to make sure you don't.

3 How could you ever think of bringing

4 someone into my apartment?

5              **STEVE**

6 It wasn't my fault.

7              **PAM**

8 It never is. (BEAT.) Alright ...

9 alright. Look, Steve. I'm willing to

10 forget this ever happened if you will

11 promise me not to bring anyone home

12 again. *END OF 1ˢᵗ THIRD*

13              **STEVE**

14 Alright.

15              **PAM**

16 And you mustn't see Karen again

17 either.

18              **STEVE**

19 Alright.

1           PAM

2 I can't afford for anyone to find out

3 anything personal about me. Listen

4 Steve, I'm going to tell you a

5 secret, if you promise not to tell

6 anyone.

7           STEVE

8 I promise.

9           PAM

10 I'm working at B&R, but I'm getting

11 paid a lot more by someone else to

12 pass on important information.

13          STEVE

14 You're a corporate spy?
   —— END OF 2ND THIRD
15          PAM

16 That's right, Steve. So, now you see

17 how important it is for me that no

18 one asks questions. I have built up a

1 life here. No family; no connections;

2 no questions. Okay?

3                    STEVE

4 I'm sorry Pam. I would never do

5 anything to hurt you.

6                    PAM

7 I know you wouldn't, Steve. But,

8 sometimes you don't think about what

9 you do.

10                    STEVE

11 I know. I'm sorry. You're the only

12 family I have.

13                    PAM

14 You'll always have me. So, if

15 anyone ... anyone at all, asks you

16 any questions, don't say anything.

17                    STEVE

18 Okay.

19

1               PAM

2 Come on. I'll get your pillow and

3 blanket. (PAM EXITS.)

4 CUT TO: F. S.

5               *ACT 5 SCENE 2*

6 (HOSPITAL WAITING ROOM. NATALIE AND

7 DAYNA ARE SITTING TOGETHER AT A

8 TABLE. SONJA AND KEVIN ARE TALKING IN

F. S.

9 THE CORNER. MALCOLM ENTERS WITH ED.

10 NATALIE RUNS OVER TO MALCOLM.)

11               NATALIE

12 What's your blood type?

13               MALCOLM

14 My blood type?

15               NATALIE

16 Yes, what is it?

END OF 1ST THIRD

17               MALCOLM

18 AB negative. Why?

1                    NATALIE

2 Kevin, get the doctor.

3                    MALCOLM

4 What is going on? What is this about

5 my blood type? ——— *END OF 2ND THIRD*

6                    NATALIE

7 Damon has to have a transfusion. Now!

8 If not he's going to die.

9                    MALCOLM

10 Damon has my blood type?

11                    KEVIN

12 There is no time for conversation.

13 Come with me. (MALCOLM STARES AT

14 NATALIE FOR A SECOND AND THEN FOLLOWS

15 KEVIN. ⌐ *F.S.* ED WALKS OVER TO HER.)

16                    NATALIE

17 You didn't tell him.

18

1              ED

2 I didn't think that it was my place

3 to tell him.

4              NATALIE

5 You're right. I'll have to do it.

6              ED

7 He did tell me something.

8              NATALIE

9 What?

—— END OF 1ST THIRD

10              ED

11 He was with Damon last night.

12              NATALIE

13 What do you mean he was with Damon?

14              ED

15 They were out drinking together.

16

1              NATALIE

2 Drinking? What are you talking about?

3 Damon is too young to drink. Doesn't

4 Malcolm know that?

— END OF 2ND THIRD

5              ED

6 Yes. And he feels terrible about it.

7 He tried to get Damon to go home, but

8 he wouldn't. So, he took his car

9 keys.

10             NATALIE

11 He left Damon by himself. Drunk.

12             ED

13 Natalie, he feels terrible about it.

14             NATALIE

15 I can't believe he did this.

16             ED

17 Well, it's done. Right now you'd

18 better come up with a reason for not

1 telling him that Damon is his son.

2 (CLOSE ON NATALIE.)

3 CUT TO: *F.S.*

4               *ACT 5 SCENE 3*

5 (JAMES' LIVING ROOM. NIGHT. SHANNON

6 IS SITTING ON THE SOFA READING. THERE

7 IS A KNOCK ON THE DOOR.)

8               SHANNON

9 I'll get it, Helga. (SHE GOES TO THE

F.S —⌐ (It's obvious she is talking
10 DOOR.) I'm sorry. It's very late.
       to someone who just
11               TERESA entered the room.)

12 Please, Shannon. Let me in. I need to

13 talk to you.

14               SHANNON

15 There is nothing to talk about.

16

1                    TERESA

2 Shannon, please. I haven't been

3 drinking. Let me speak to you.

4 (SHANNON LETS HER IN.)

5                    SHANNON

6 Would you care for some coffee?

7                    TERESA

8 No, thank you. Tell me ... tell me

9 where Greg is?

10                   SHANNON

11 I swear, Mrs. Reed. I don't know.

12                   TERESA

13 I have to know. Is he alright?

14                   SHANNON

15 Mrs. Reed, I haven't heard from him.
   — END OF 1ST THIRD
16                   TERESA

17 (SHE TRIES TO CONTROL HER TEMPER)

18 Please, don't lie to me Shannon. I

19 know that you know where he is.

1                    SHANNON

2 I think you'd better leave now.

3                    TERESA

4 Please, Shannon. I'm sorry. Please

5 help me.

6                    SHANNON

7 I didn't lie to you. I don't know

8 where he is.

9                    TERESA

10 Why didn't he come to me?

11                    SHANNON

12 Because you wouldn't understand.

13                    TERESA

14 How could I not understand? I'm his

15 mother.

16                    SHANNON

17 That's probably why you wouldn't

18 understand.

1                    TERESA

2 It's drugs, isn't it?

—— END OF 2ND THIRD

3                    SHANNON

4 Yes, there are some people

5 threatening him.

6                    TERESA

7 Oh, my God. I knew it all along. I

8 should have gotten him treatment.

9                    SHANNON

10 Didn't you hear me? His life is in

11 danger.

12                    TERESA

13 We could have gone to the police. I

14 could have helped him.

15                    SHANNON

16 That's right. Call the police. Have

17 him put away. All you would do is

18 humiliate him.

19

1               TERESA

2  He needs me.

3               SHANNON

4  If you had been there when he needed

5  you, he wouldn't be in trouble now.

6               TERESA

7  (THEY ARE SHOUTING NOW.) Why would

8  you say that to me? I have always

   F.S ⌐
9  loved him. (TRES ENTERS AND STANDS IN

10 THE DOORWAY.)

11              SHANNON

12 (UNABLE TO CONTROL HER ANGER.) Maybe

13 if you had let him know that he

14 wouldn't have run away. You parents

15 are all the same. You talk about

16 love, but you never talk about

17 respect. You just don't give a damn.

18 (SHE RUNS OUT OF THE ROOM.)
      —— F.S.

1                    TERESA

2 (TURNING TO TRES.) How could she say

3 these things to me?

4                     TRES

5 She's upset. She didn't mean it.

6                    TERESA

7 She should at least tell me where he

8 is.

9                     TRES

10 Mrs. Reed, she doesn't know where he

11 is. She's worried sick about him.

12                    TERESA

13 I'm sorry. I'm just so frightened.

— END OF 1ST THIRD

14                    TRES

15 (GOES OVER AND PUTS HIS ARMS AROUND

16 HER.) I know. (SHE STARTS TO EXIT.)

17                    TERESA

18 (SHE TURNS BACK.) I'm sorry about

19 last night.

1                    TRES

2 Forget it. It's alright.

3                    TERESA

4 I know I shouldn't drink. I can't.

5 You were so kind to me.

—— *END OF 2ND THIRD*

6                    TRES

7 You really don't have to say

8 anything.

9                    TERESA

10 I'm sorry if I hurt you.

11                   TRES

12 I don't know what you are talking

13 about.

14                   TERESA

15 It's alright. I understand. (SHE

16 TURNS AND WALKS AWAY.)

17 CUT TO: *F.S.*

18

```
1               ACT 6

2  (PAM'S APARTMENT. LATE NIGHT. STEVE

3  IS ON THE SOFA, TOSSING, TURNING AND

4  TALKING IN HIS SLEEP. HIS AGITATION

5  BUILDS.)

6               STEVE

7  No ... I won't ... I won't tell ... I

8  promise ... Don't ... Please don't

9  hurt me ... Please ... Stop ... (HE

10 IS NOW VERY LOUD.) STOP ... NO!!!!

11             PAM

12 (SWITCHING ON THE LIGHTS. SHE RUNS
              F.S.⌐
13 INTO THE ROOM│GOING OVER TO STEVE.)

14 Steve ... Steven ... (SHE SHAKES HIM

15 AS HE STILL STRUGGLES TO WAKE. HE IS

16 STILL SCREAMING.)  Stevie ... (SHE

17 SHAKES HIM MORE.) Honey, snap out of

18 it. Steve. (HE OPENS HIS EYES.)

19
```

1               STEVE

2 Mama ... Mama ... Don't let them hurt

3 me.

4               PAM

5 (WIPING HIS FACE.) Oh God, Stevie ...

6 Stevie, baby.

7               STEVE

8 (LOOKING AT PAM.) Mama? Is that you

9 Mama?

10              PAM

11 (SHE BEGINS TO CRY.) Yes, darling.

12 Mama's here. You're gonna be okay,

13 baby. (TEARS POUR DOWN HER FACE.)

14 Mama will take care of you.

—— END OF 1ˢᵗ THIRD

15              STEVE

16 It hurts, Mama. It hurts.

17

1               PAM

2 I know honey. I know. Let me get you

3 some milk.

4               STEVE

5 No, Mama. No! Don't leave me. Don't

6 leave me alone. It's dark. Don't

7 leave me alone.

8               PAM

9 I won't honey. Mama won't leave you.

10              STEVE

11 I didn't mean to do it Mama.
  —— END OF 2ND THIRD
12              PAM

13 I know, honey. I know you didn't.

14              STEVE

15 They make me so angry.

16              PAM

17 Who does? Who makes you so angry?

18

1               STEVE

2 They all do. I don't want to do it,

3 but they make me.

4               PAM

5 It's all right, Stevie. I won't let

6 them do it. (STEVE IS BECOMING MORE

7 AND MORE CALM AS PAM ROCKS HIM IN HER

8 ARMS, AND SINGS.) Hush little baby,

9 don't say a word, Mama's gonna buy

10 you a mocking bird. And if that

11 mocking bird don't sing, Mama's gonna

12 buy you a diamond ring. (PAM IS

13 CRYING PROFUSELY.)

14 FREEZE FRAME / ROLE CREDITS

15 FADE TO BLACK.
        —— F. S.

## *About*
## *The Weatherford Group*

THE WEATHERFORD GROUP, located in the heart of Hollywood, is re-establishing "the old studio system" in today's television industry. Russ Weatherford and his partners -- Dean Regan, Curtis Platte, Ed Wermund and Damon Berg -- have created a professional home base for actors, writers, directors and producers who require a studio model in which to perfect their crafts. The Weatherford Group is comprised of three components:

THE WEATHERFORD GROUP -- A PRODUCTION STUDIO;
THE WEATHERFORD GROUP ARTIST STUDIO AND
THE HOLLYWOOD REPERTORY COMPANY *AT COLE PLACE*.

THE WEATHERFORD GROUP is a production company specializing in "blueprinting" -- testing new scripts for creativity and commercial viability. The Weatherford Group has a project book with approximately 50 screenplays, television pilots and stage plays in the works at any one time. The Weatherford Group currently produces the cable soap opera *SECRETS*, with an estimated audience of two million people in Southern California. Under the executive direction of Russ Weatherford, *SECRETS* is taped on The Weatherford Group's fully-equipped soundstage, in a unique environment with actors functioning behind the cameras as well as on the set.

THE WEATHERFORD GROUP ARTIST STUDIO is specially designed for the television and film professional. The Weatherford Technique is taught to working professionals. The basis of the technique is two-fold: (1) storytelling is the artist's most important social responsibility, and (2) acting is a "science," not just an "art." As a science, there are formulas to follow to achieve the necessary results: getting into the 3% minority of those consistently employed within the entertainment industry.

Russ Weatherford has trained professionals on both coasts at Actor's in Advertising in New York, Professional Artists Group in Los Angeles and finally THE WEATHERFORD GROUP ARTIST STUDIO.

THE HOLLYWOOD REPERTORY COMPANY *at Cole Place*, under the direction of Dean Regan, is housed at The Weatherford Group. The ensemble consists of 30 invited artists who collectively choose their performance material and perfect their craft in a live stage medium.

# About
# The Author:
# Russ Weatherford

The road to Hollywood can be quite a challenge for a young man from South Carolina; but Russ Weatherford seems to have accepted each challenge as if it were a gift. Born and reared in Union, South Carolina, "Rusty" always loved to perform and often recruited the neighborhood children as his "supporting cast". But it wasn't just a passing fancy. After receiving his B.A. in journalism from The University of South Carolina, Weatherford went on to spend four years with the U.S. Air Force where he wrote and directed theatre and television for the American Forces Radio and Television Service. Even after being accepted to Law School, Russ was unable to deny his love of "story-telling". He changed his graduate program to Theatre and went on to receive his M.A. in Theatre from U.S.C.

What followed was a litany of stage productions that carried him throughout the East, and finally, on to New York City. His list of Theatre credits continued to grow and soon Russ began what would be seven years of Soap Opera roles. He was seen on "The Doctors", "The Edge of Night", "One Life to Live", and "All My Children" playing the character of "Russ Sloan" for four years.

When Weatherford left the soaps, he developed his writing, direction and production talents, as well as his teaching ability. It has long been sneered: "those that can, do; and those that can't, teach." Russ Weatherford's proven them wrong. He is in constant demand as a lecturer for seminars throughout the United States. The most requested topics of his lecture series include: "The Structure of Story-Telling," "The Road to Make-Believe," "Script Analysis," and "Screen Writing". He has taught from New York, to Orlando, to Texas, and on to Hollywood. Weatherford also pulled from his acting talents and teaching abilities to direct not only his current project, "Secrets", but also "The Ruth Warrick Concert Tour", "The Bob Hope Concert", "Secret Moments", and the soon to be produced "Lila McGuire".

As a producer, Russ has been Senior Vice President of Variety Productions in Dallas Texas and is now President and Senior Partner of The Weatherford Group, a production studio in Hollywood. Currently, Weatherford serves as Creator and Co-Producer of "Willie Gillis, An American Soldier", in development with Von Zernick Productions, and as Creator and Executive Producer of "September Spring", a sitcom in development with Jim Aubrey, former president of CBS and MGM/UA. Weatherford is currently developing projects for Gale Storm and Ruth Warrick. He is Co-Creator and Co-Executive Producer of "Hawke's Hawaii", a project currently in development. Russ also created and is co-producing "La Sangre Dire", a novella. For The Weatherford Group, he created "Desires", an international soap; "Carries Corner", a sitcom; and *SECRETS*, a cable daytime drama, which is currently reaching two million viewers in Los Angeles and may be seen on cable stations throughout the U.S. before 1994.

Under the umbrella of The Weatherford Group, Weatherford fosters the growth of actors, writers, and directors through the various courses offered by the Weatherford Group Artist Studio; as well as the growth of theatre in Los Angeles through The Hollywood Repertory Company *at Cole Place*. Sound like an exhausting list of responsibilities? Probably, but then again, the road to Hollywood can build a lot of stamina.

## *Order Information*

If you would like to order more copies of *Confidence & Clarity: The Complete Guide to Instant Line-Learning*, please send a check or money order for $9.95 ($10.77 for California residents) payable to "The Weatherford Group" along with your mailing information. We'll be glad to rush copies to you.

If you would like to order using your *MasterCard®* or *Visa®* please call us at 213/461-6303 (Monday-Friday, 9:00 am to 5:00 pm/Pacific Standard Time).

*We look forward to hearing from you!*

## Discount Coupon
for
**New Students**
at
**THE WEATHERFORD GROUP ARTIST STUDIO**


Bring this Coupon to
**THE WEATHERFORD GROUP ARTIST STUIDO**
for a

## 10% Discount

on Any Class or Program

**For More Information Call:
213/957-4799**

*(cut along the lines)*